404 NOT FOUND

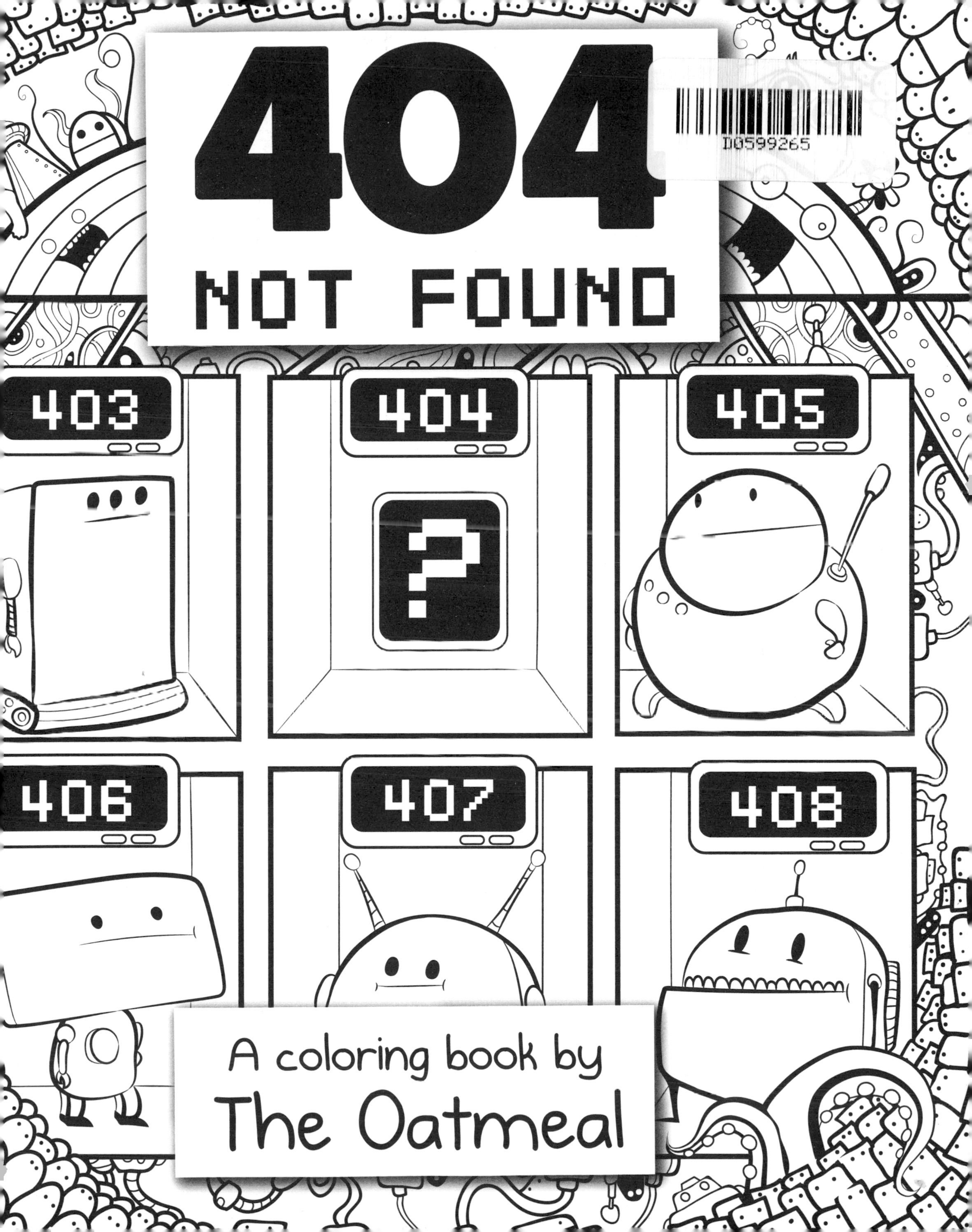
403
404
?
405
406
407
408

A coloring book by
The Oatmeal

This book is dedicated to my mom,
who taught me that it's okay to color
outside the lines,

as long as it's beautiful.

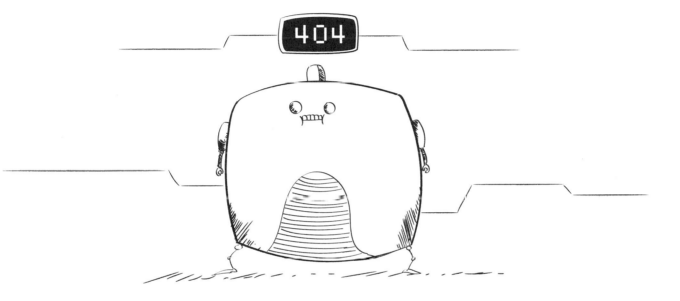

404 not found

is a story about a missing robot.

Andrews McMeel
Publishing®

a division of Andrews McMeel Universal

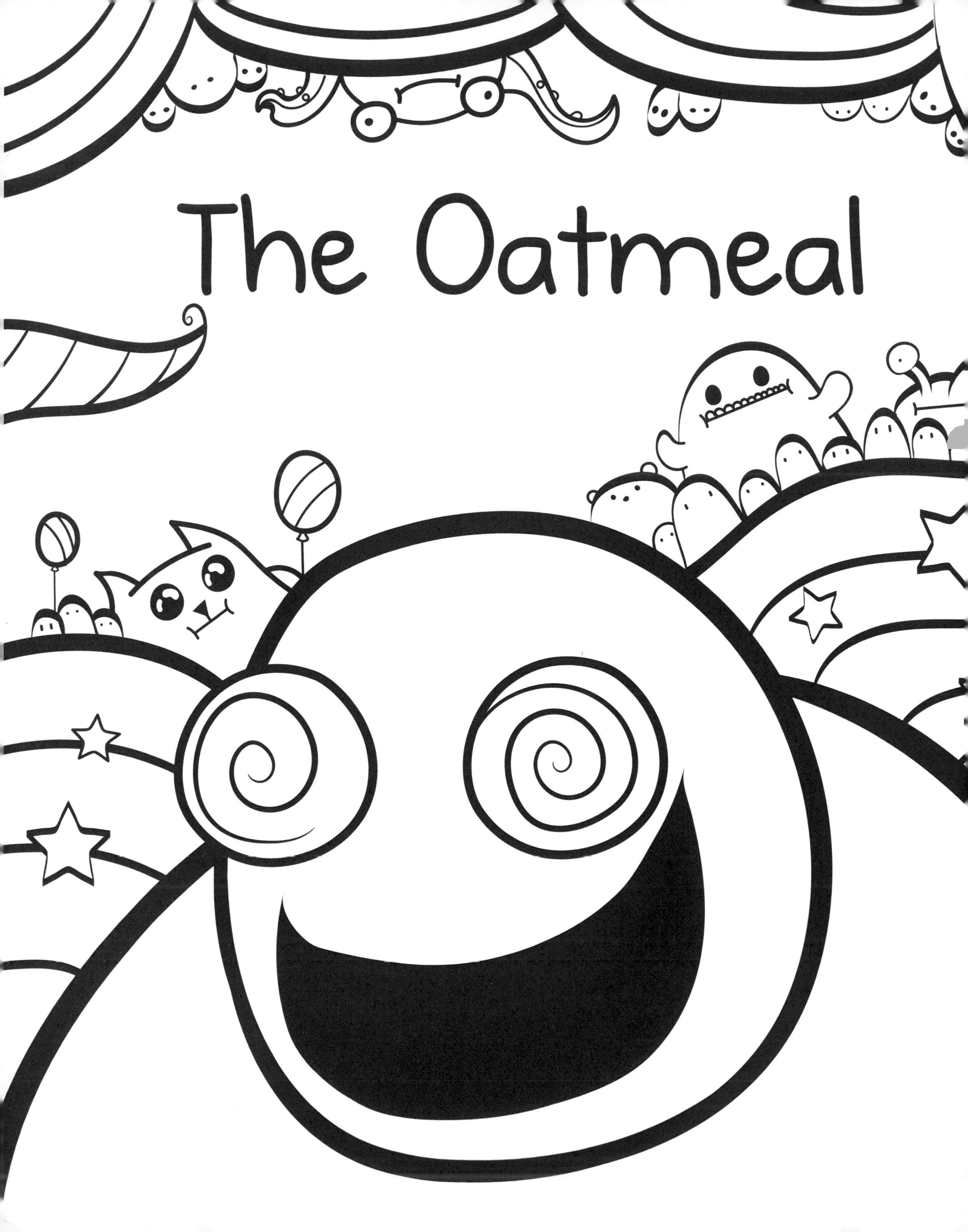
The Oatmeal

This book contains
HIDDEN OBJECTS:

☐ Undersea taco

☐ Cat in a necktie

☐ Pluto

☐ Bearded goat

☐ Party crab

☐ Dolphicorn
(dolphin + unicorn)

☐ A hairy pickle

☐ Some cat poop

☐ A winged hot dog

☐ Three-eyed cat

☐ An airborne FireSquirrel

☐ Pi

☐ The Blerch

☐ Cat in underpants

☐ One-eyed pirate pig

☐ Jibbers Crabst

☐ The bum of a gopher

☐ A pterodactyl

Every day the robots

wake

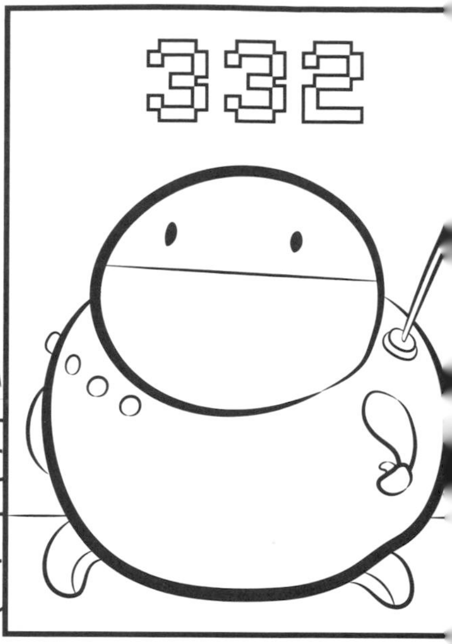
332

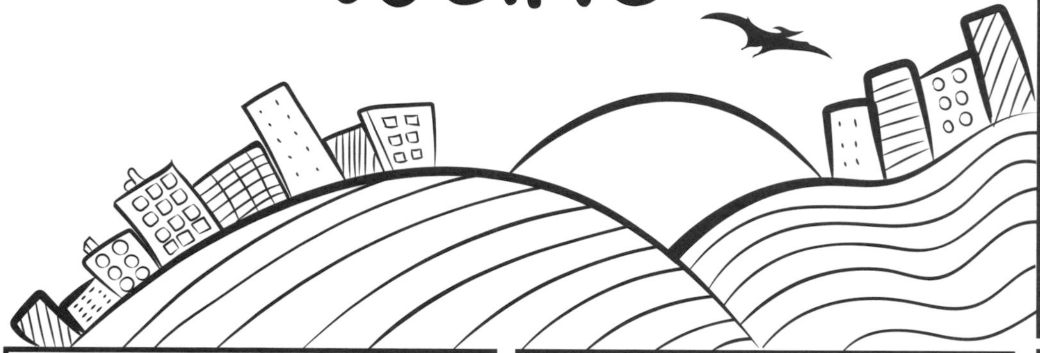

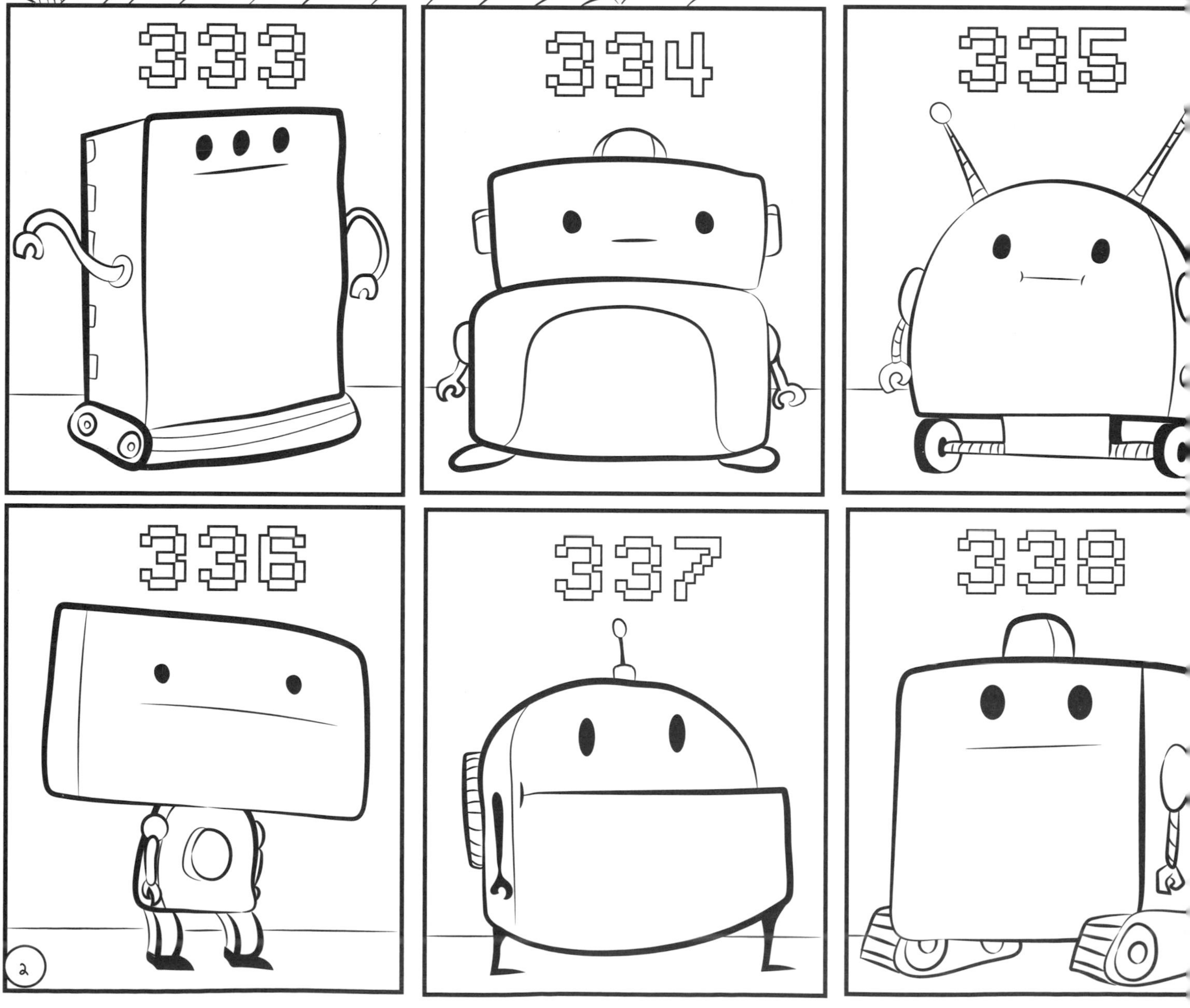
333
334
335
336
337
338

nd eat their daily

robot CAKE!

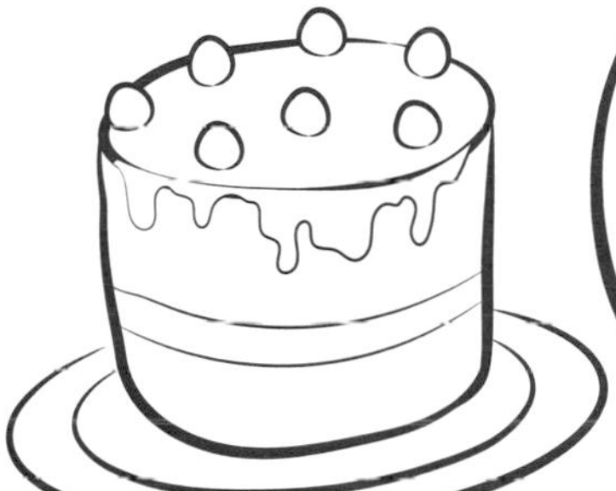

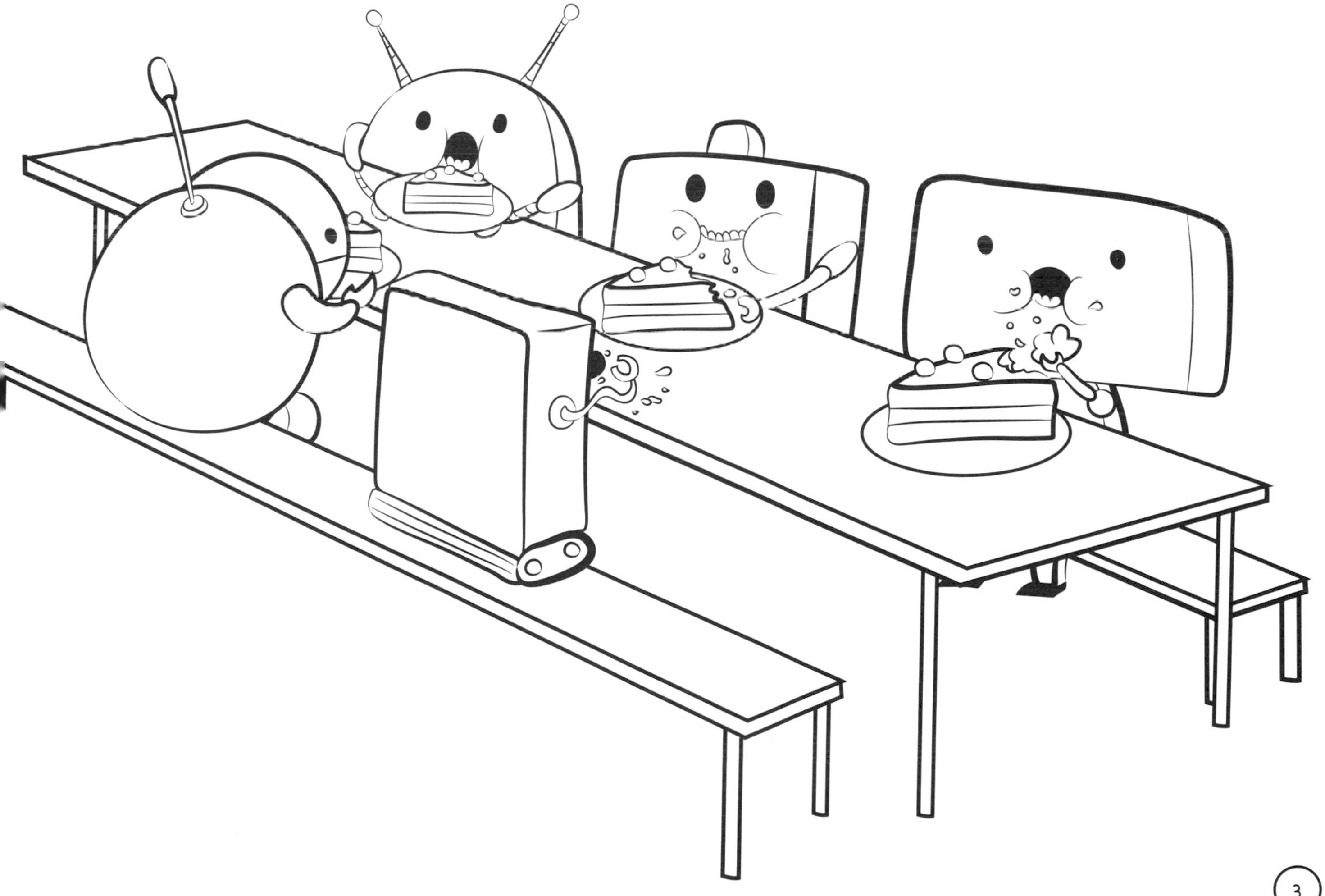

It's their job, these little

bots,

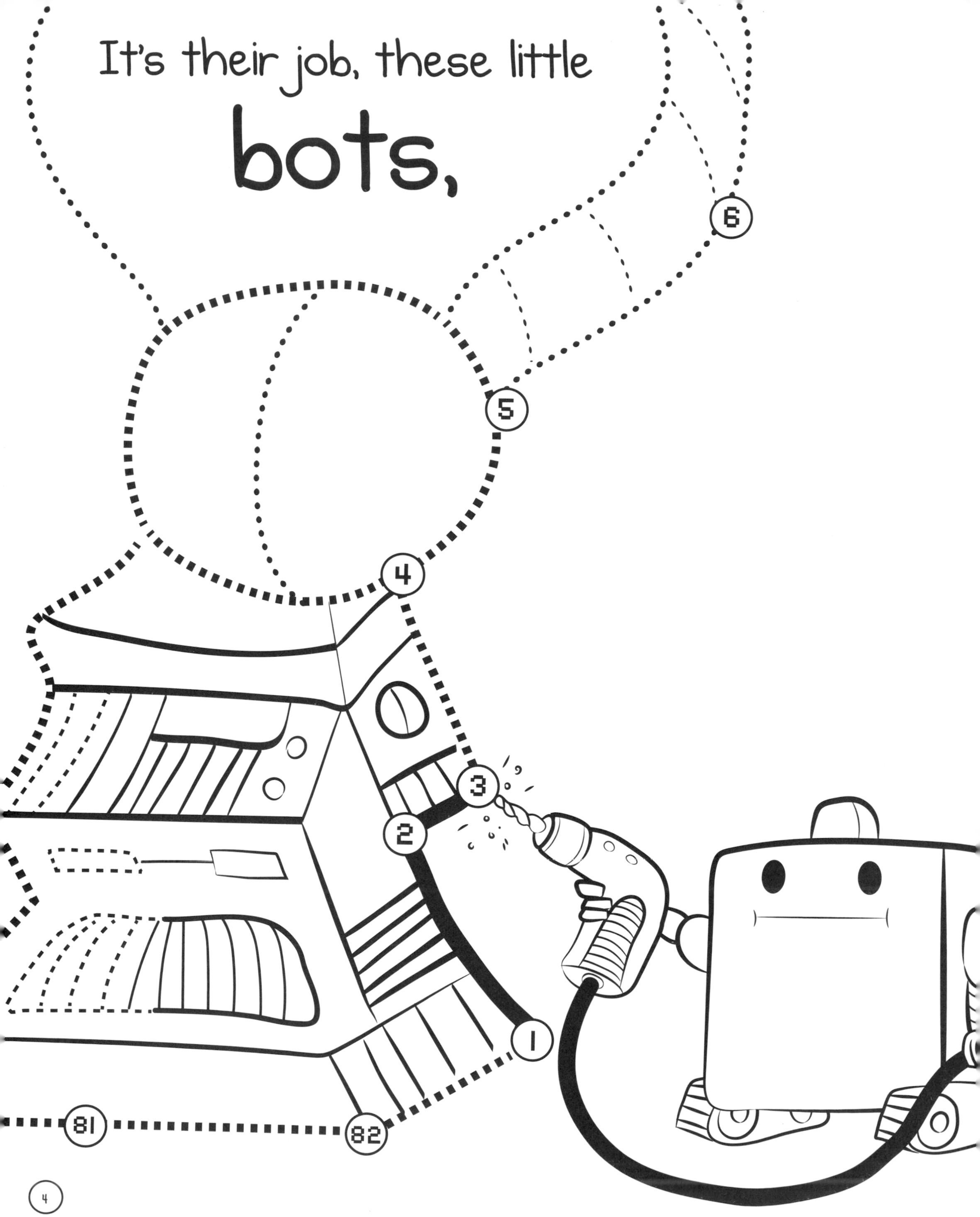
6
5
4
3
2
1
81
82

every day, to connect the
dots.

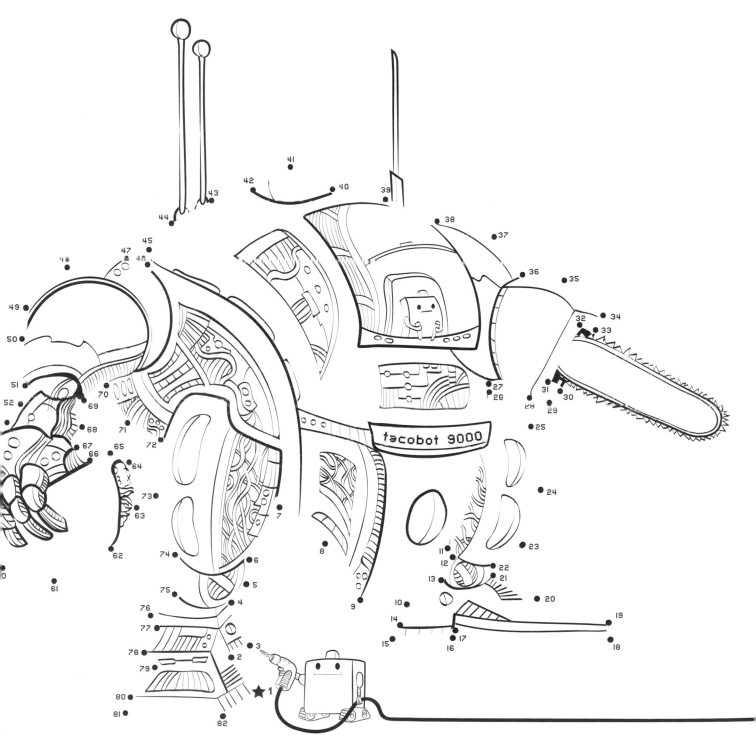

tacobot 9000

They click and whine,

beep and whir.

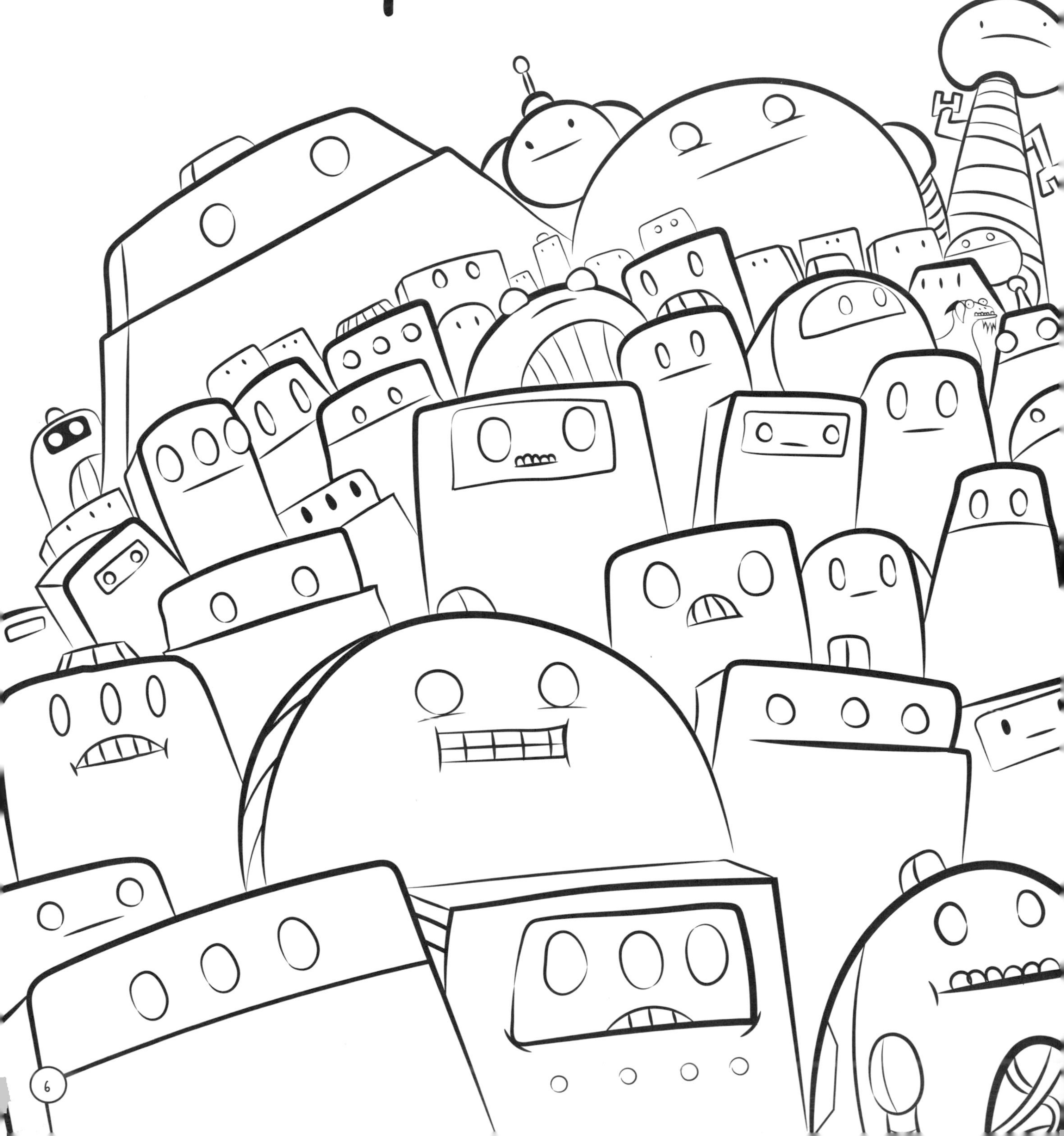

It's a mechanical garden,

a beautiful purr.

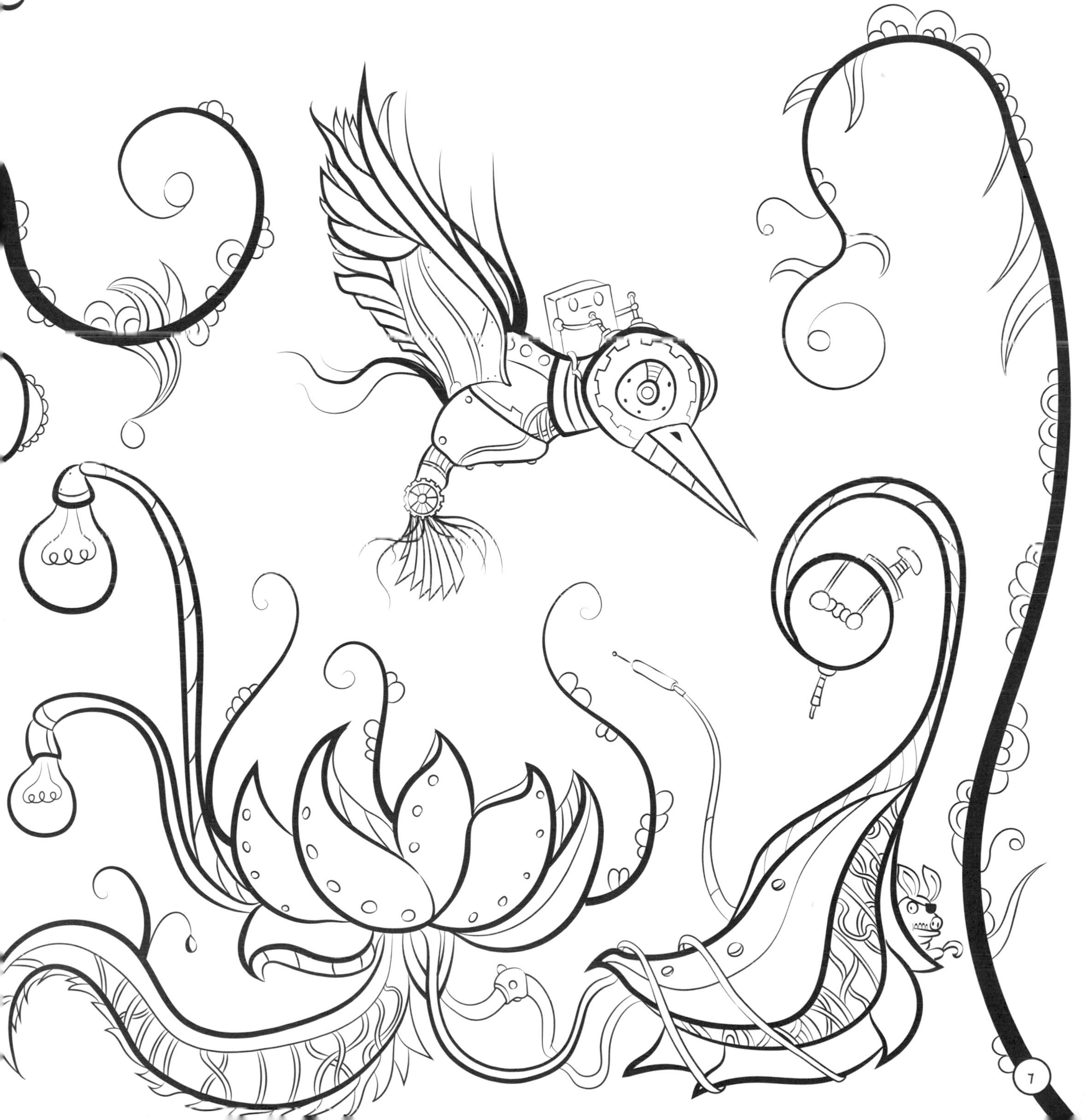

Until one morning, much to their

astound,

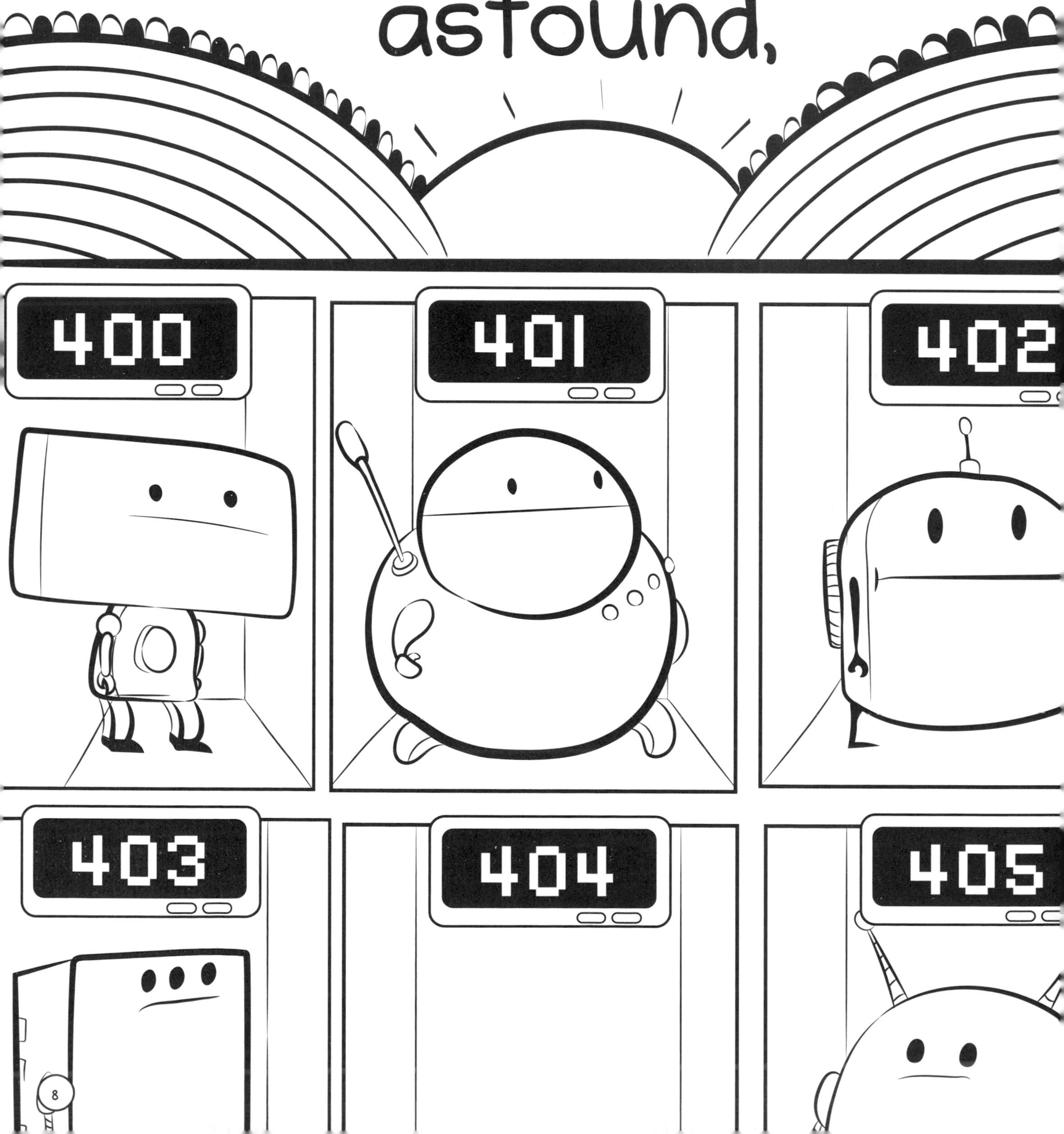
400
401
402
403
404
405

number 404,

he was not found.

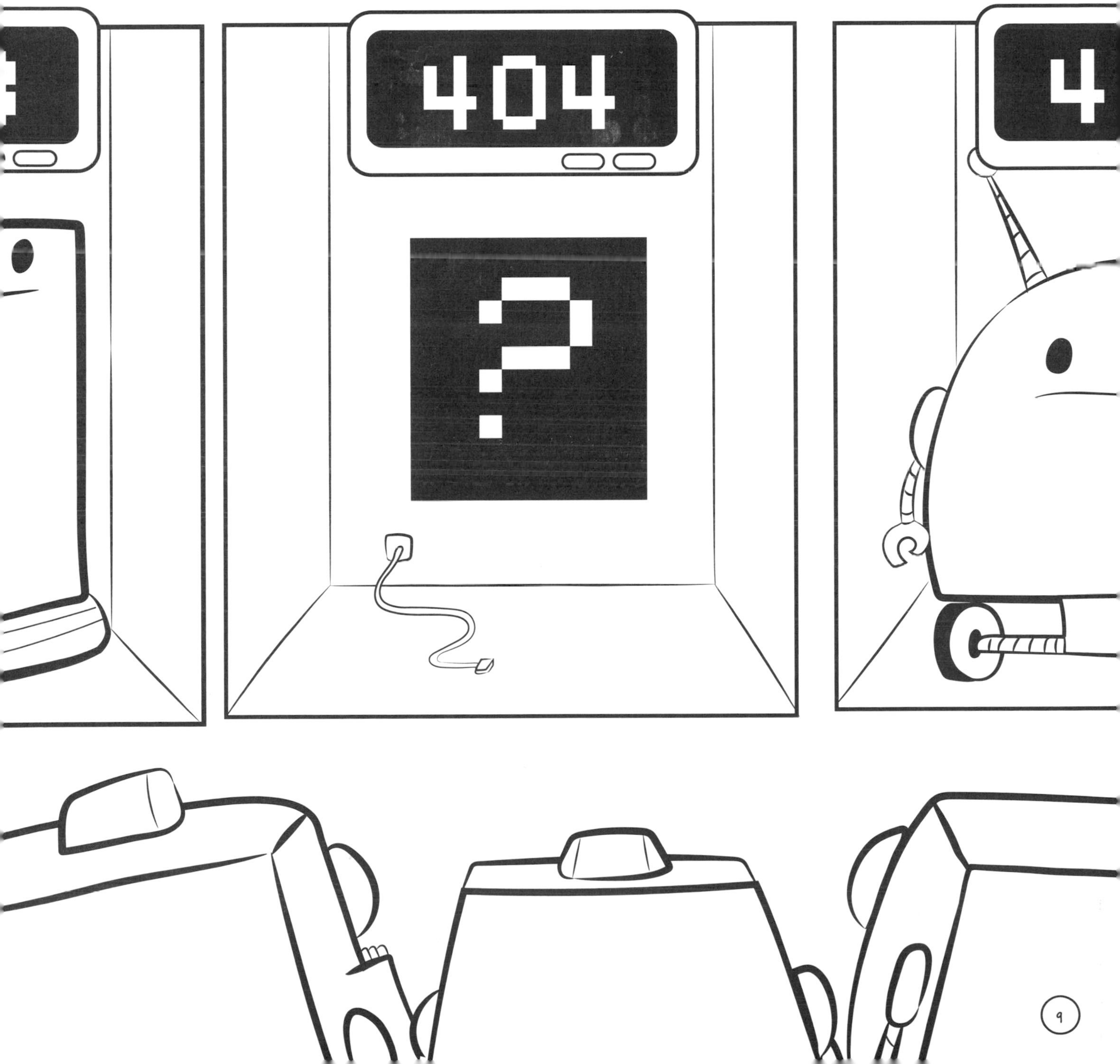
404

Perhaps he traveled
underground

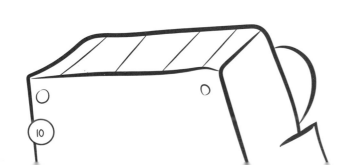

and was eaten by a

yborg gopher hound.

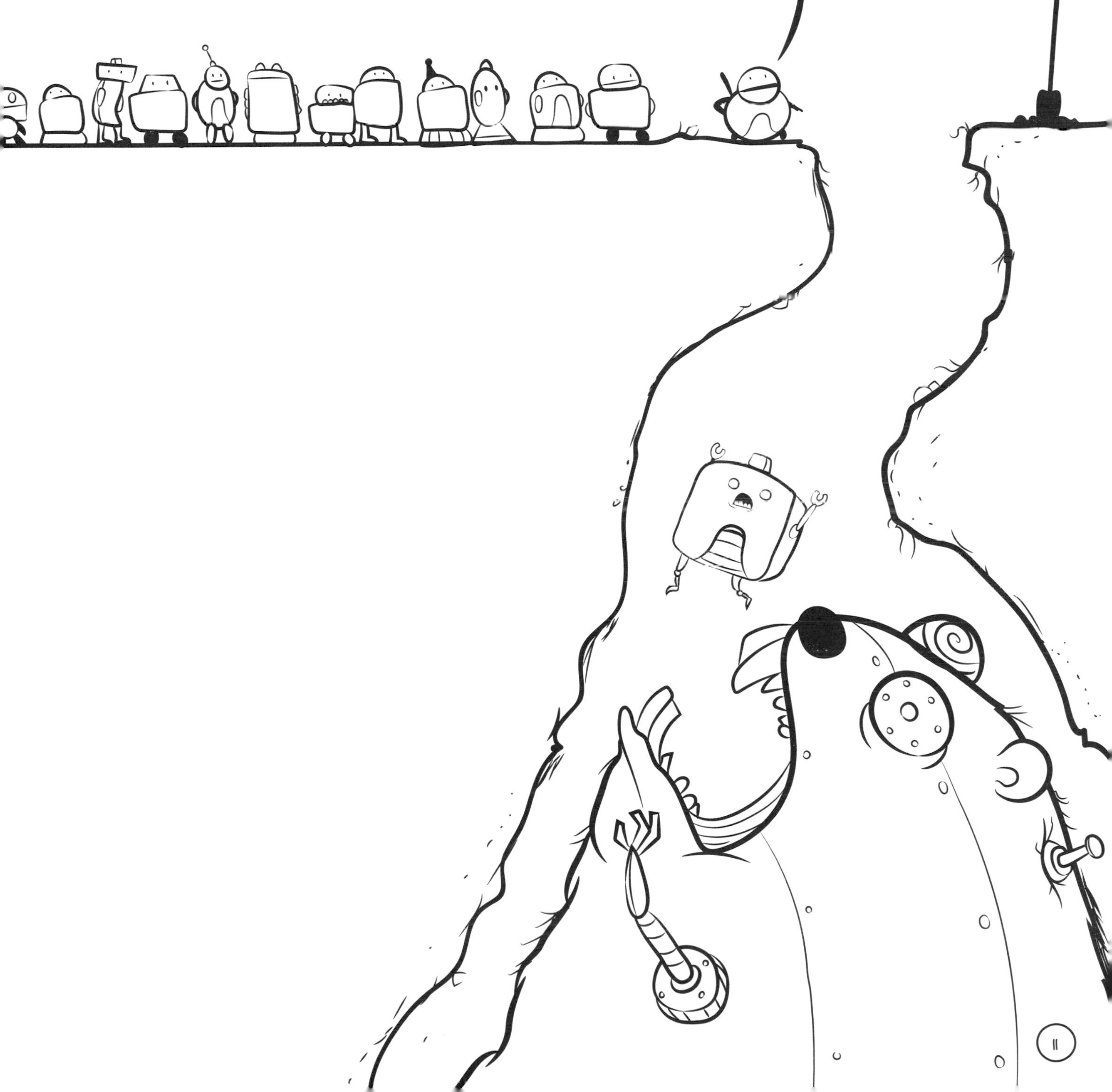

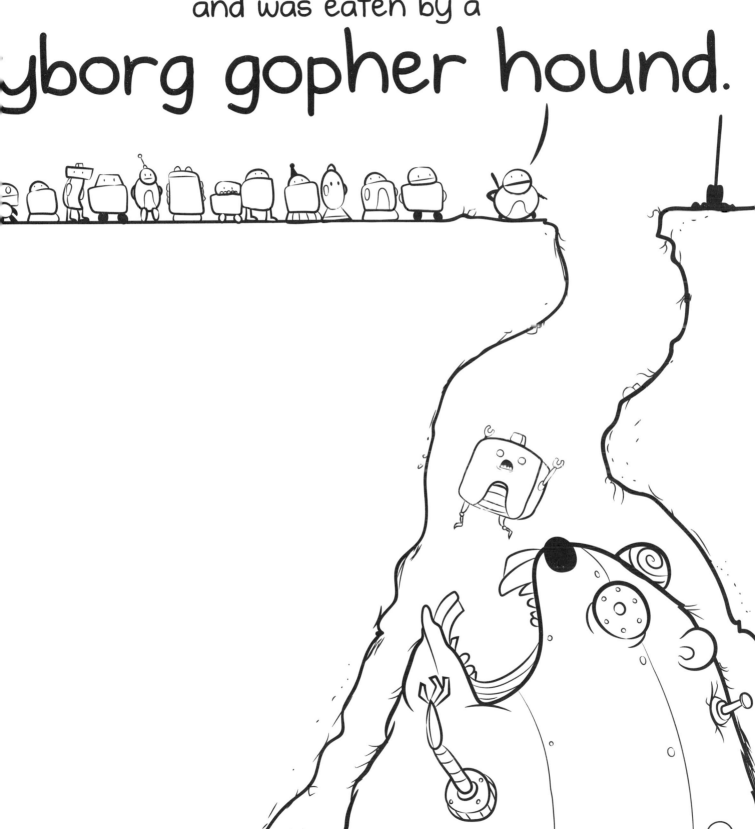

Maybe he wore his

amazing love pants

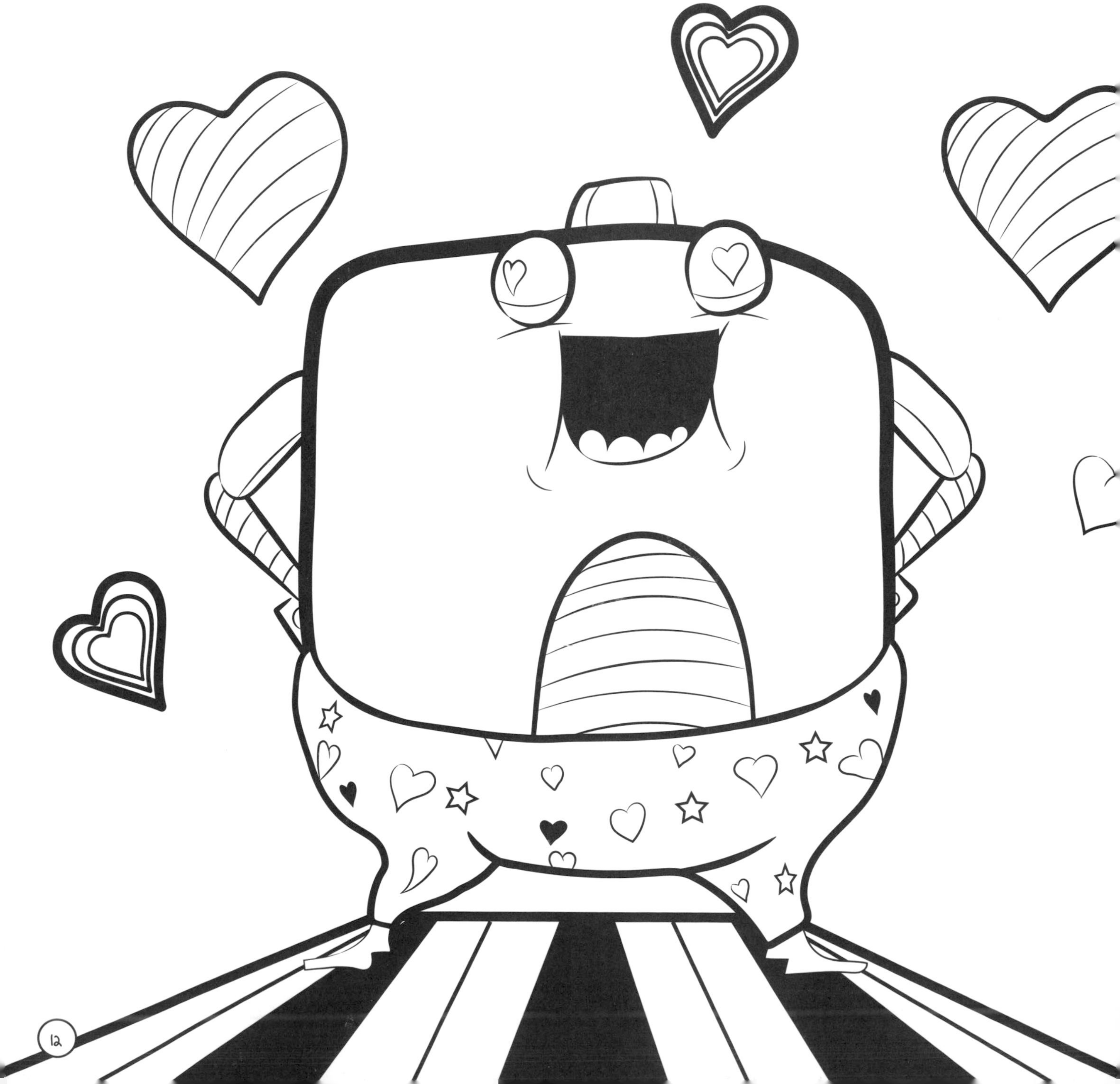

and got swept up in a

steamy robo-romance.

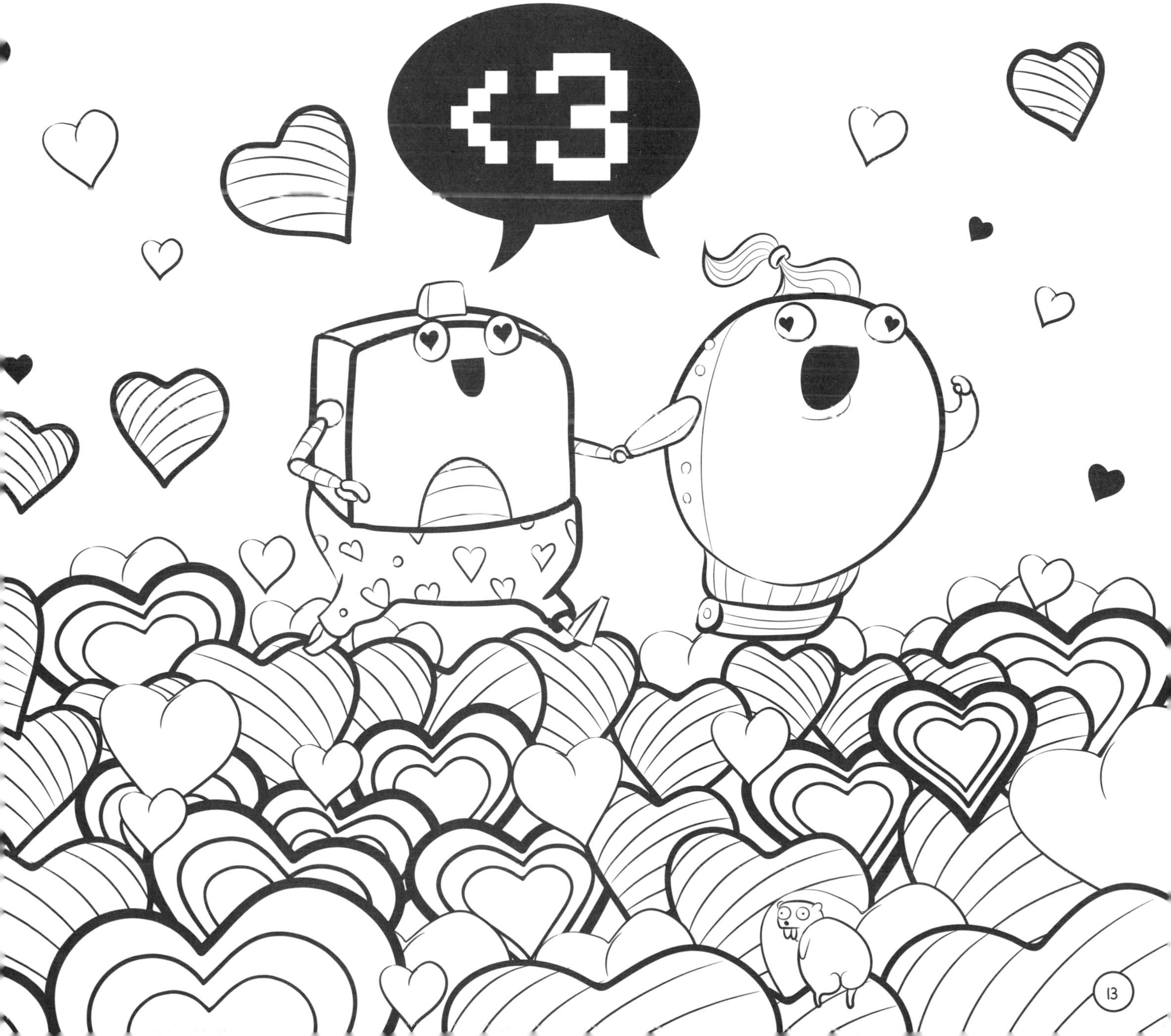
<3

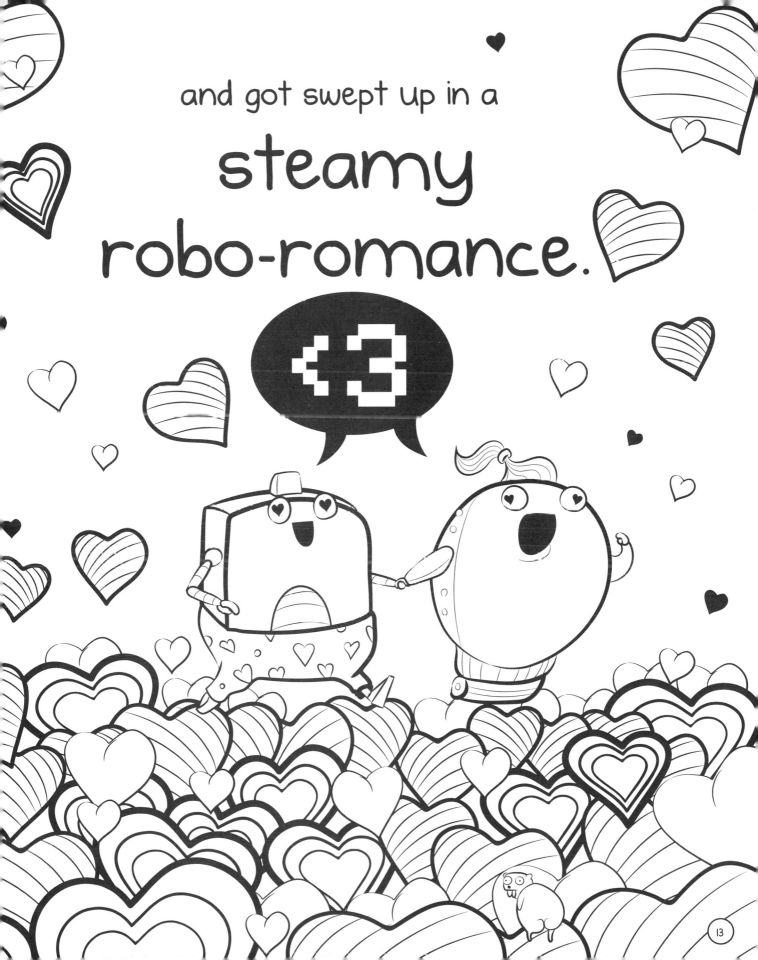

Or maybe he forgot to
check the lid

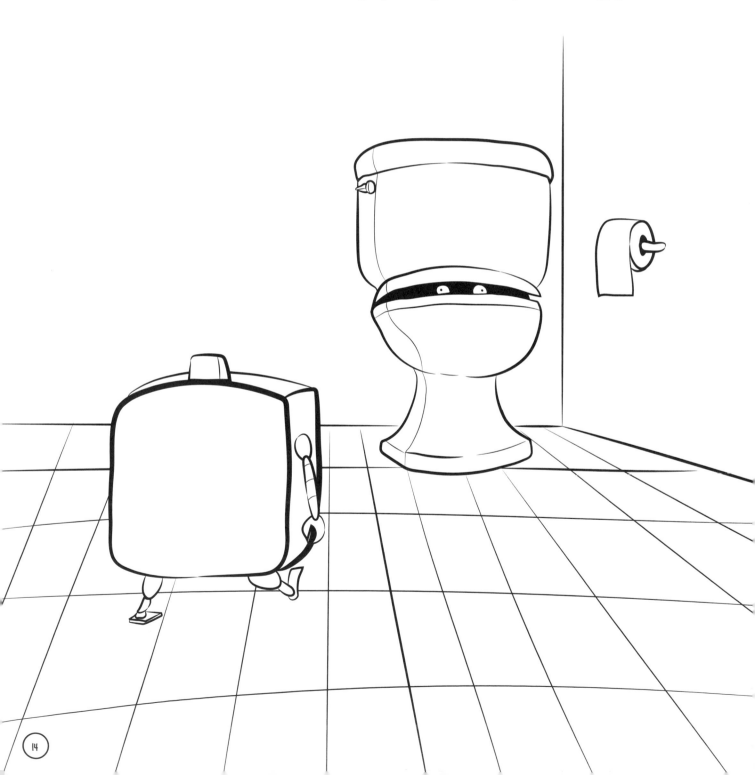

and was attacked by a

terrible toilet squid.

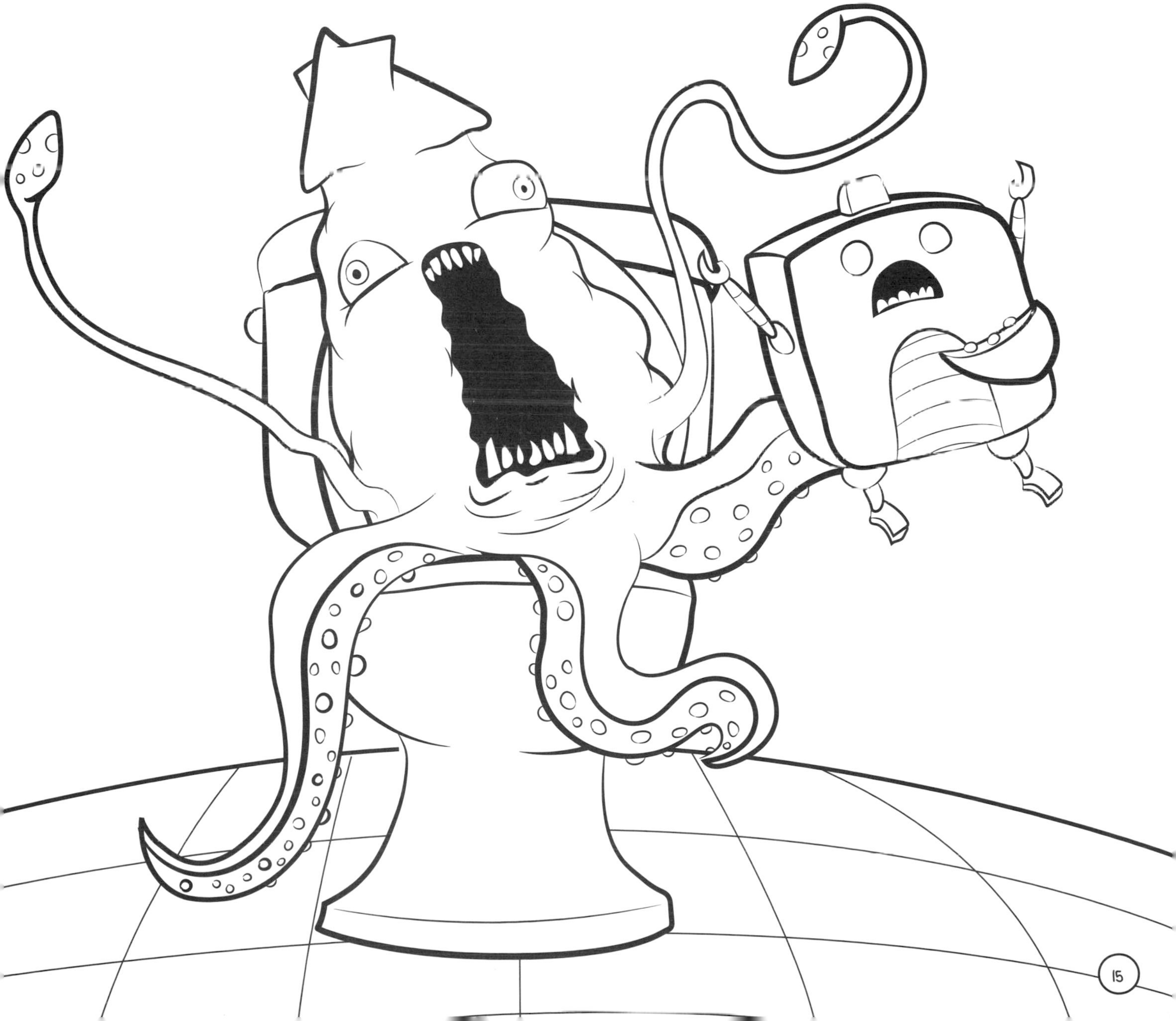

Or perhaps he made a

wish

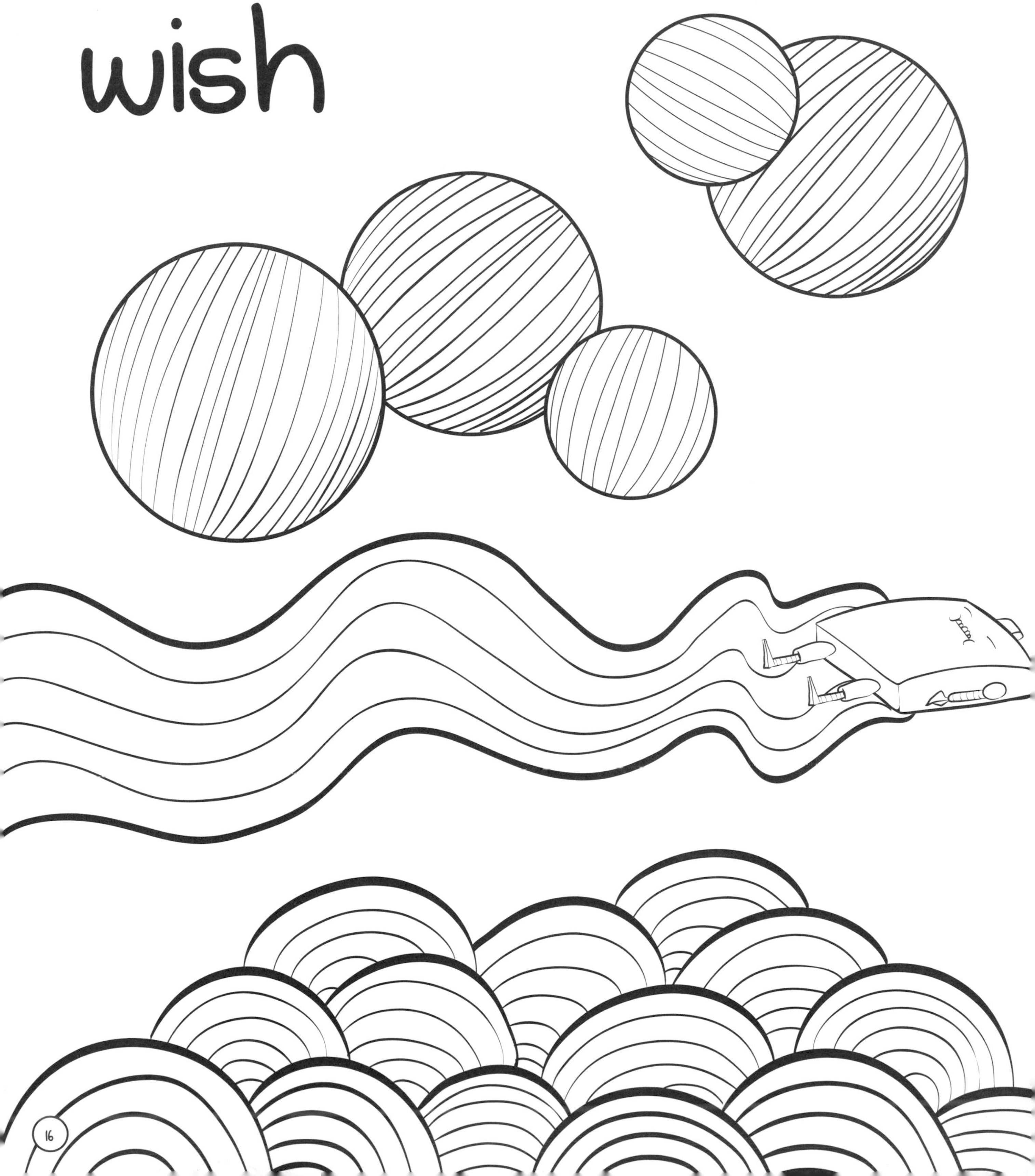

nd dreamt up an

anglerfish.

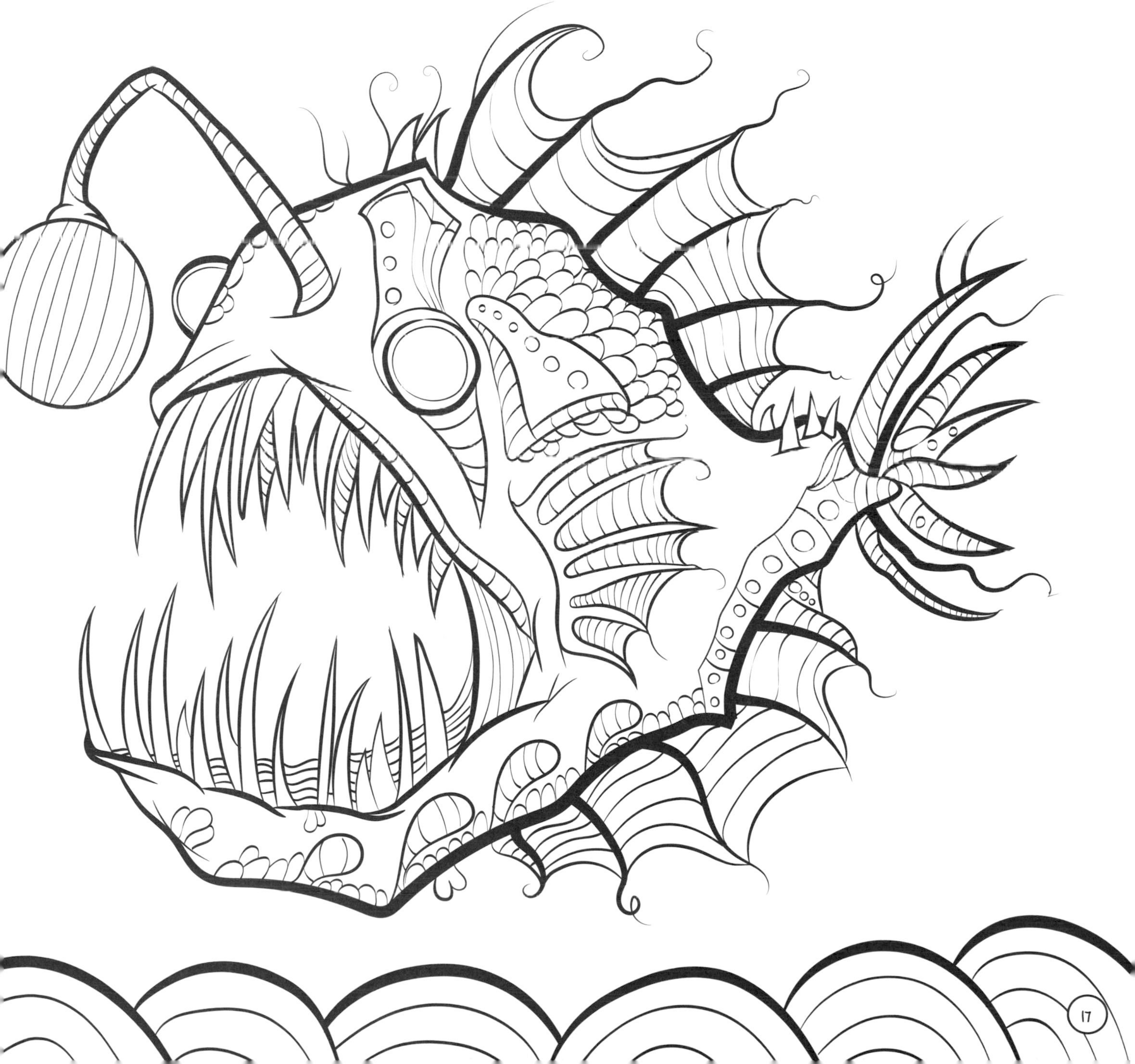

Maybe that dream became too real,

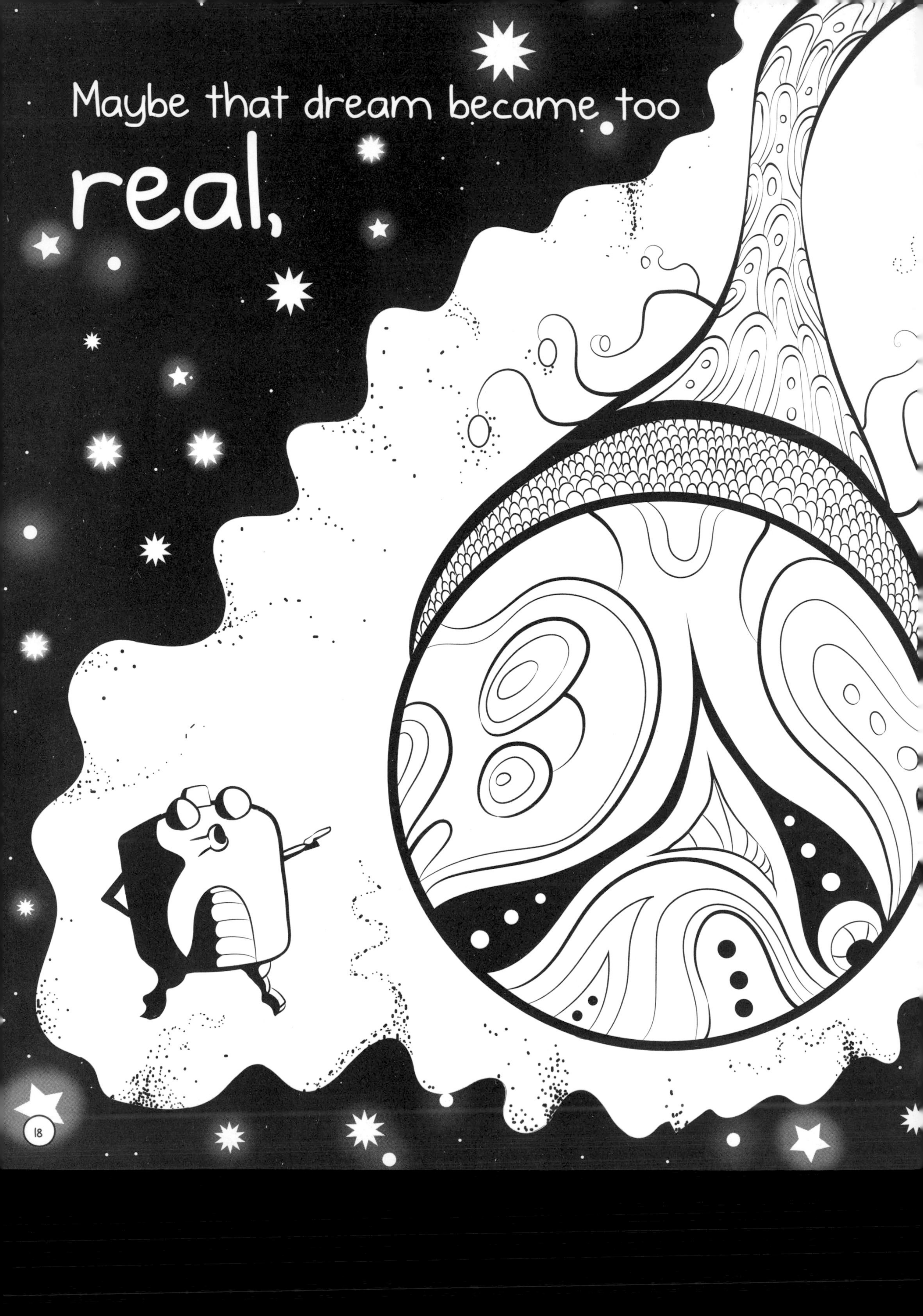

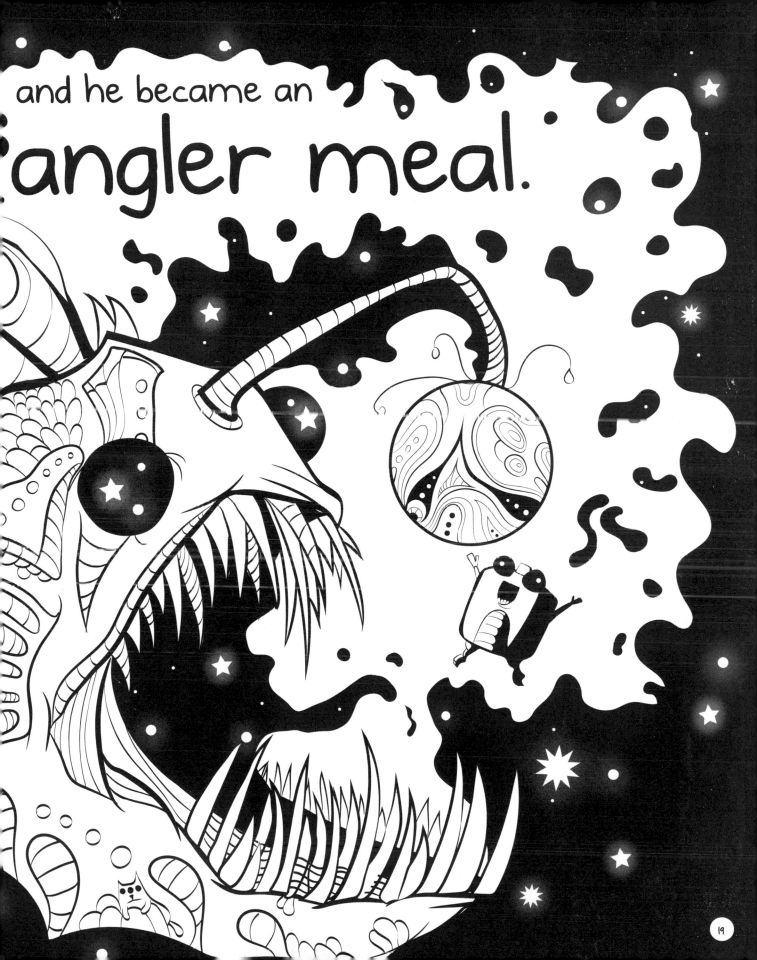

and he became an angler meal.

Or maybe things got

super weird

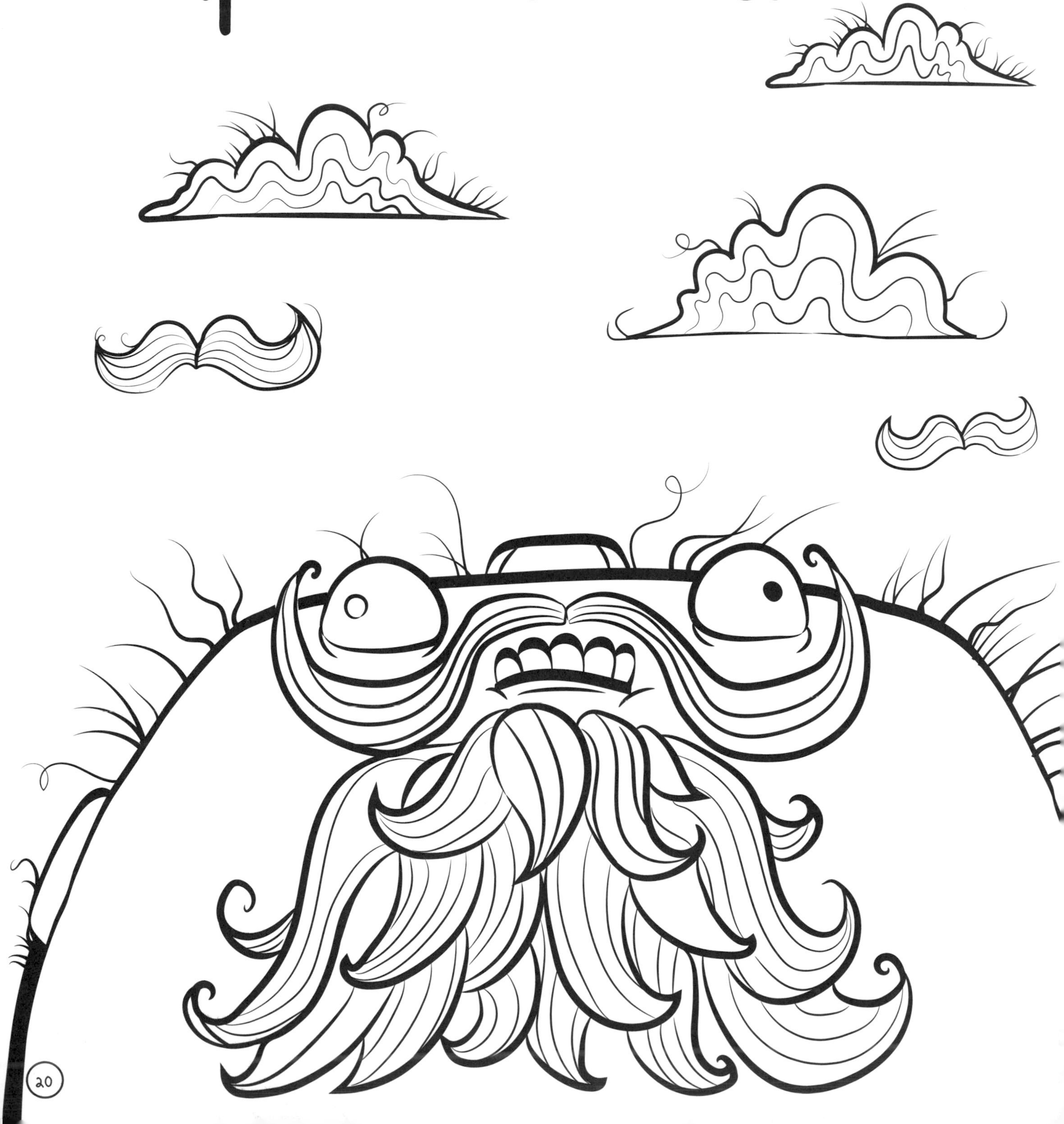

hen he hung out in the

and of beard.

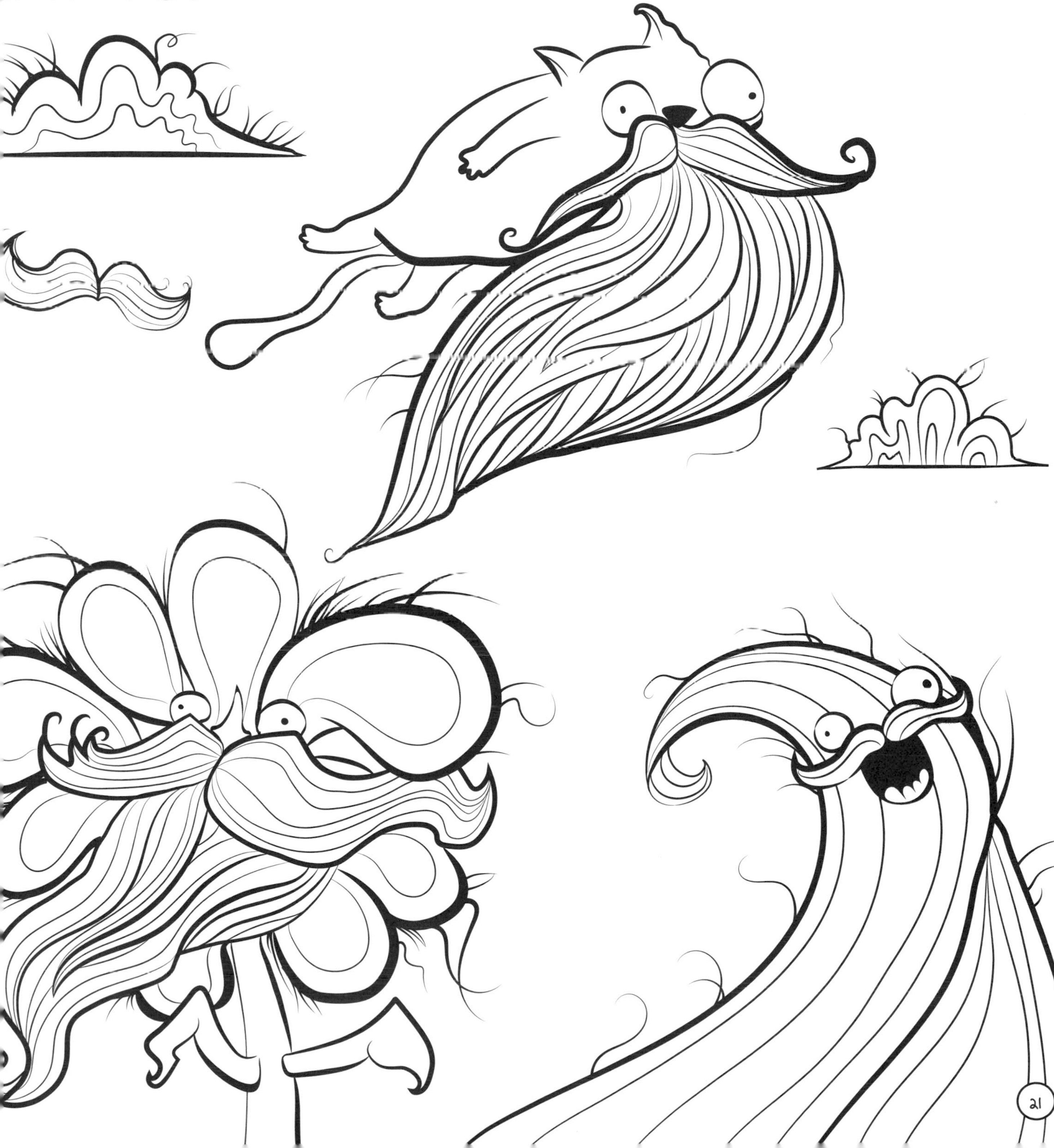

Perhaps he left this

worldly place

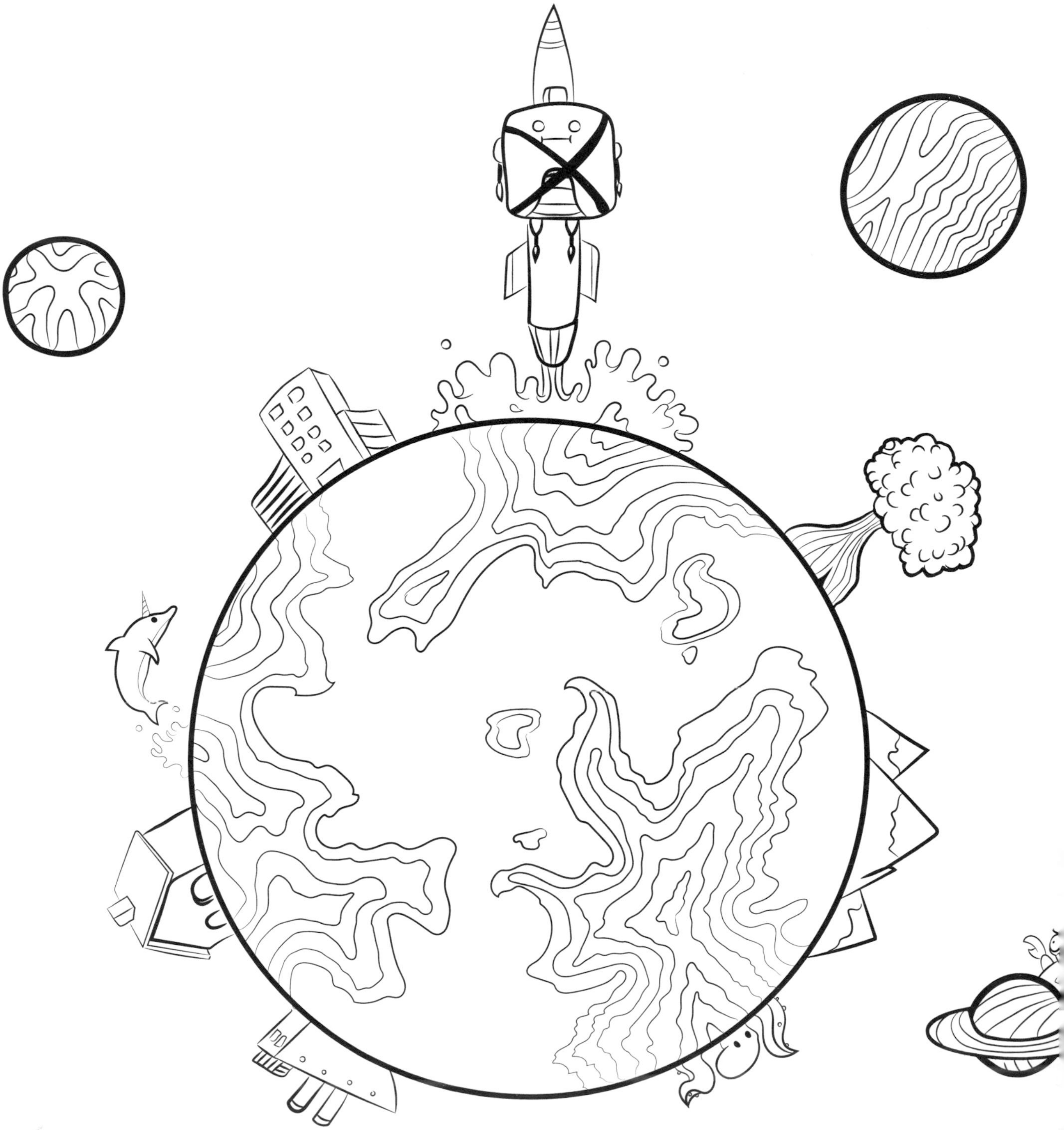

and found an

evil race

of

cats from space.

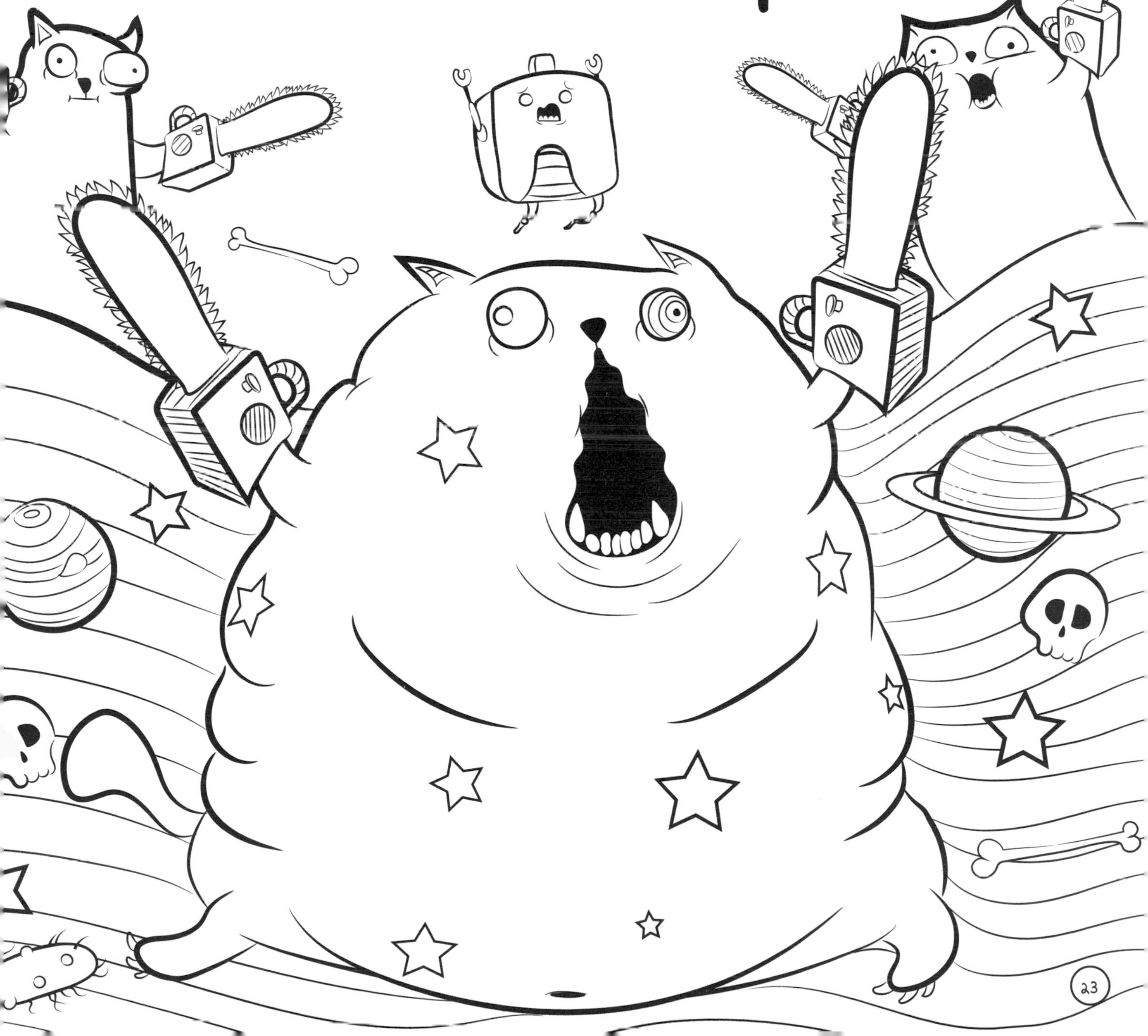

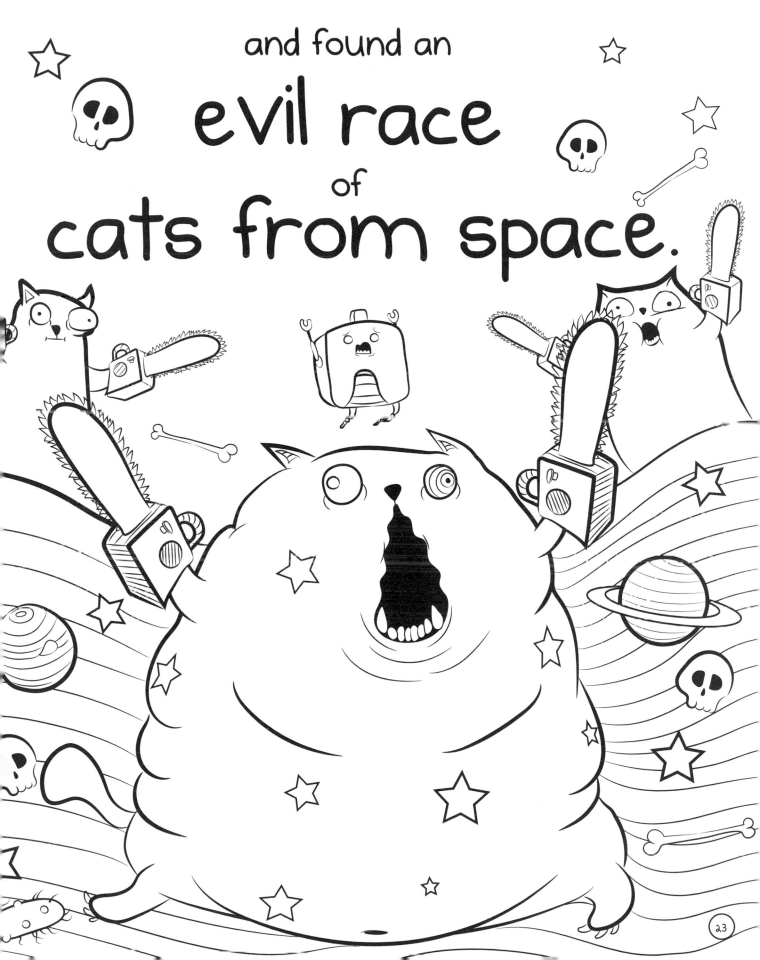

Maybe those
cats from space

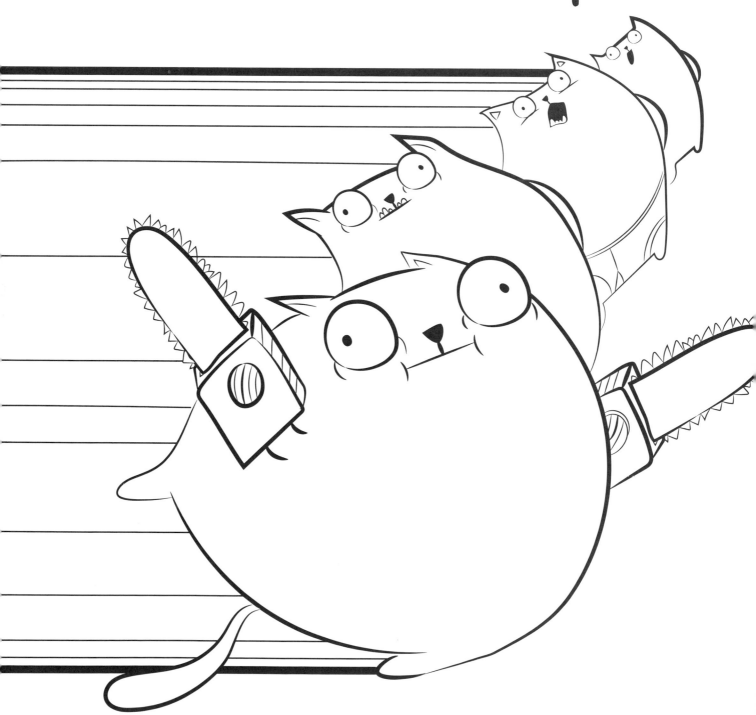

returned to this world

with murderous haste.

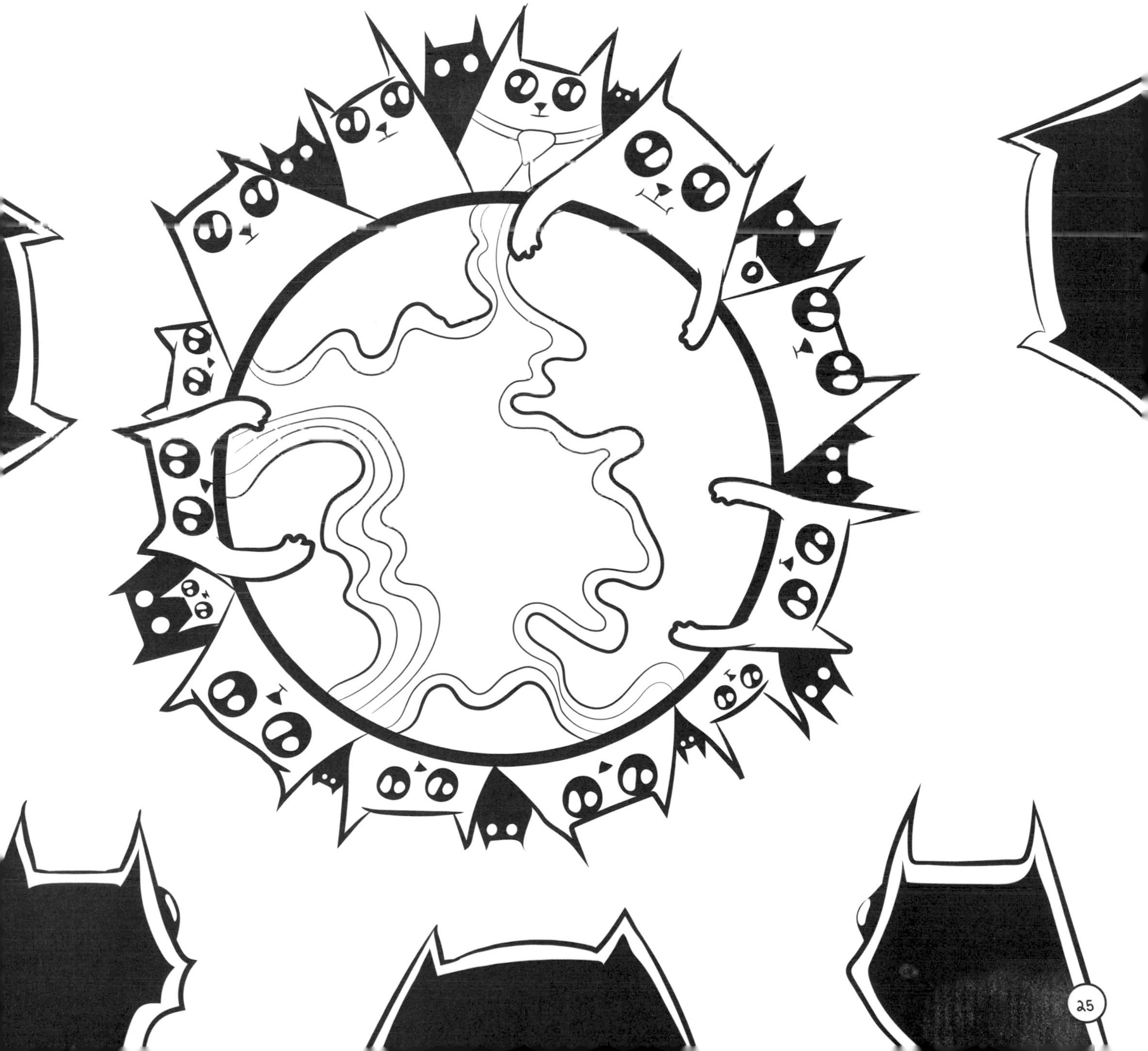

Maybe they're waiting for us to

sleep

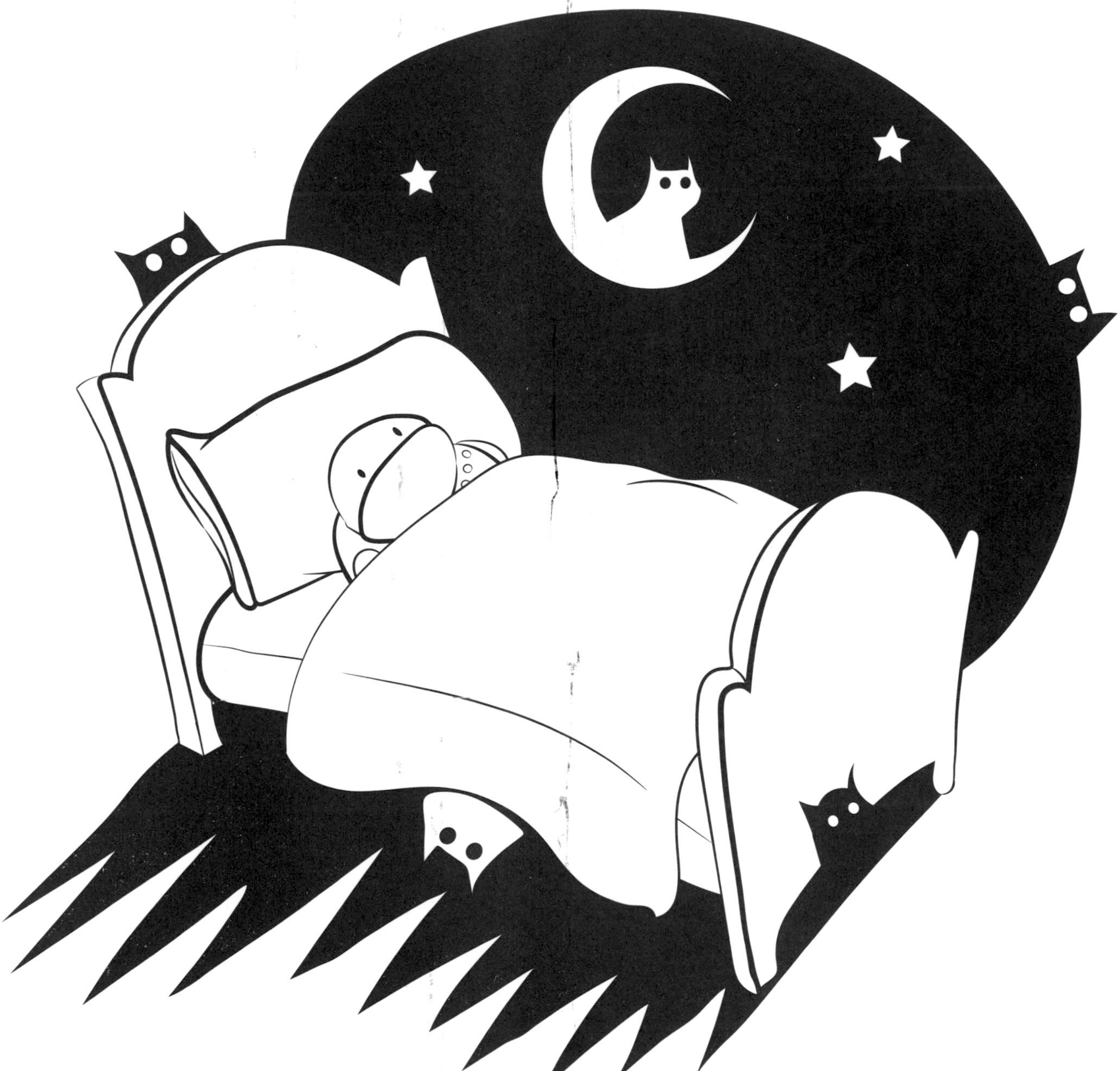

so they can feast upon our

tummy meats.

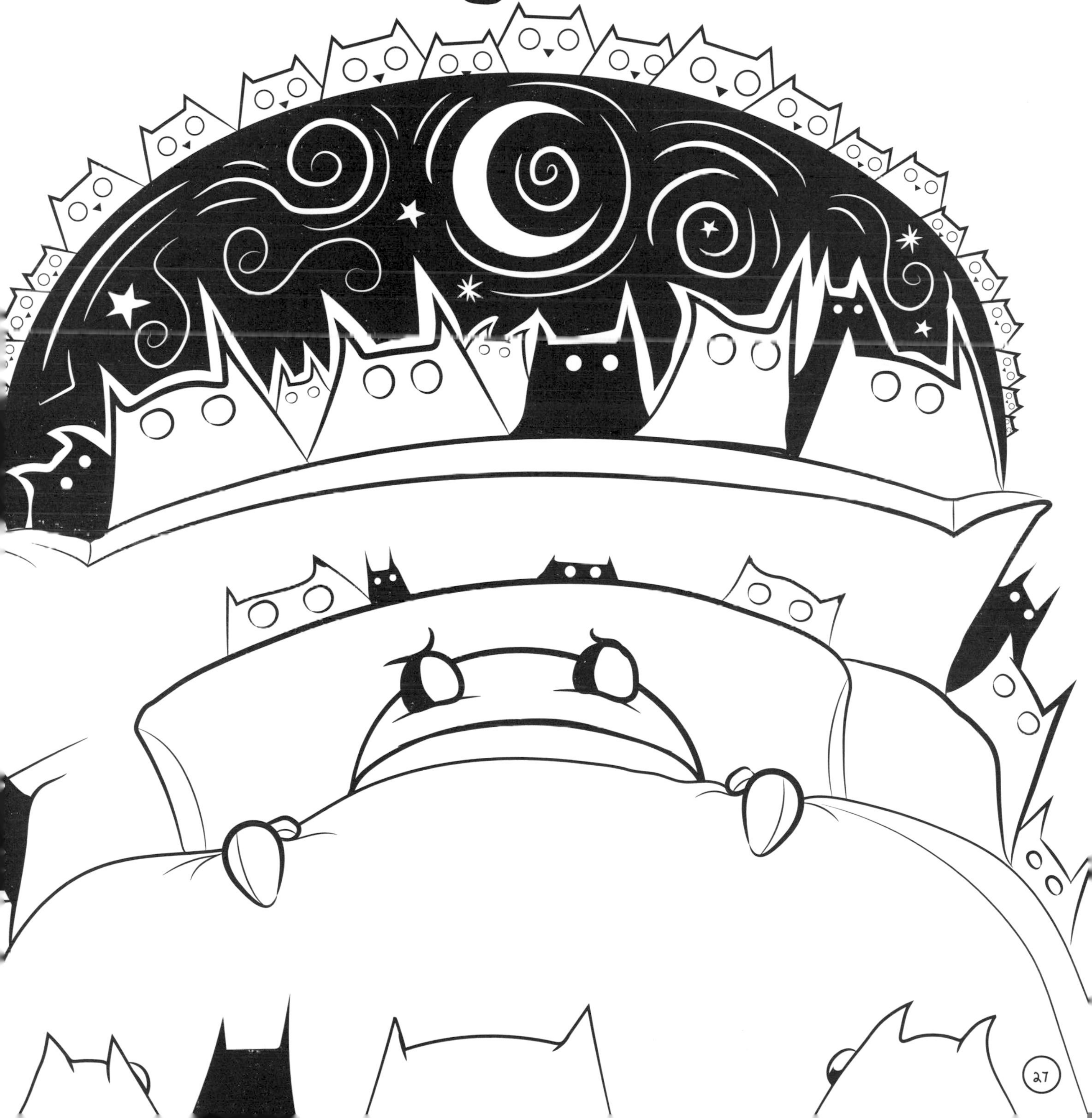

Or maybe he became a

celestial feast

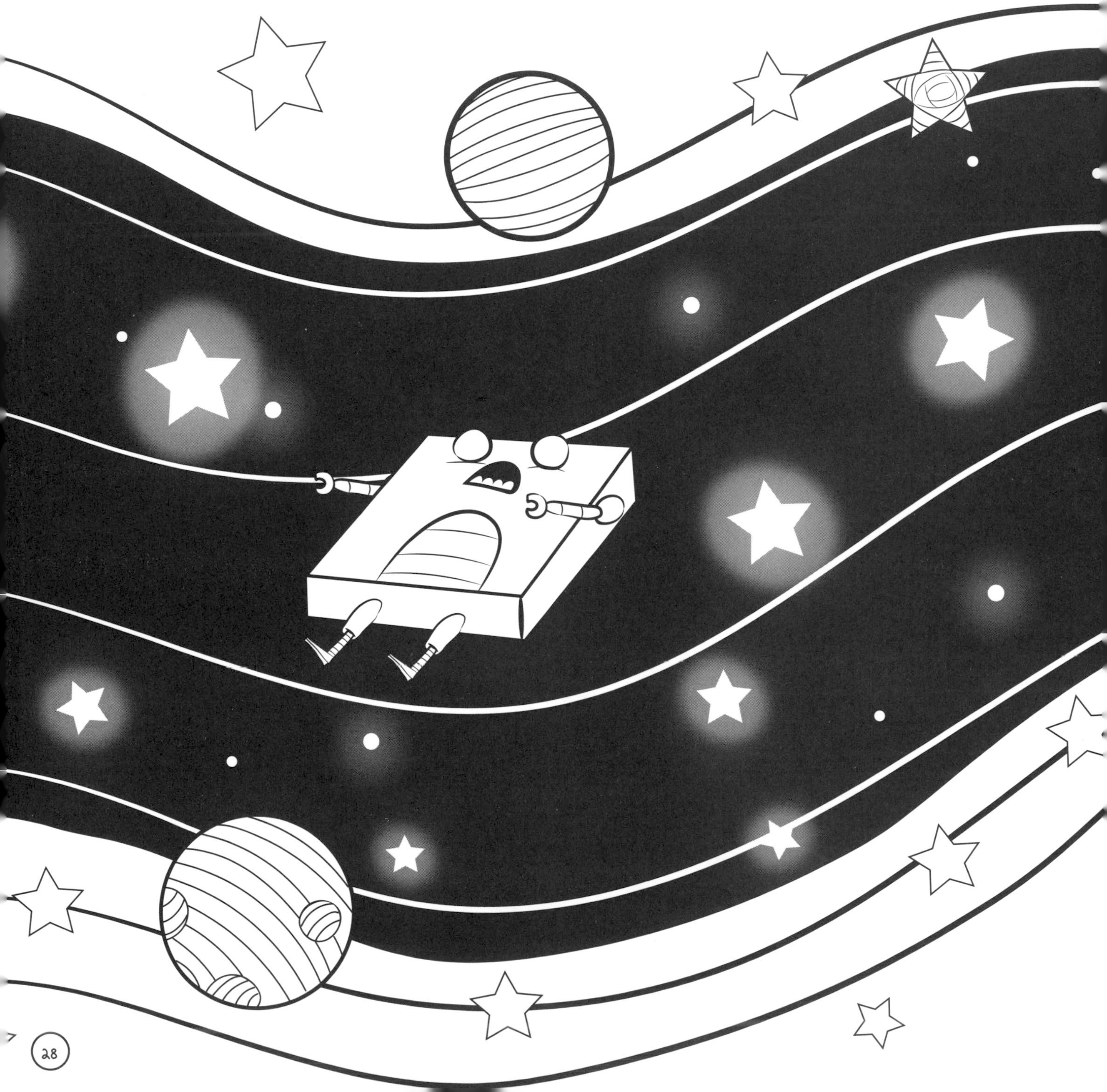

when he encountered a

black hole beast.

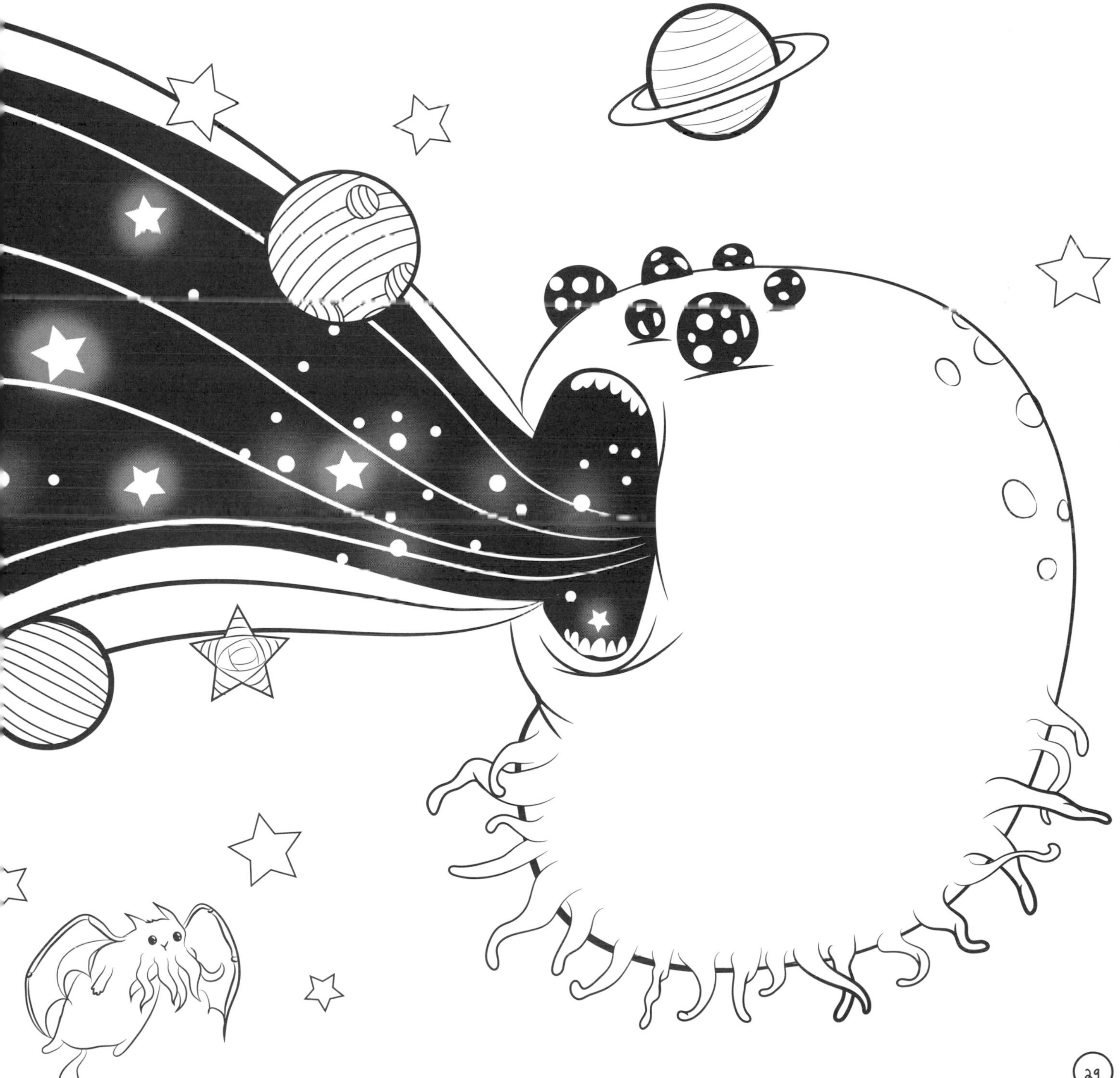

Perhaps he went searching for

Atlantis

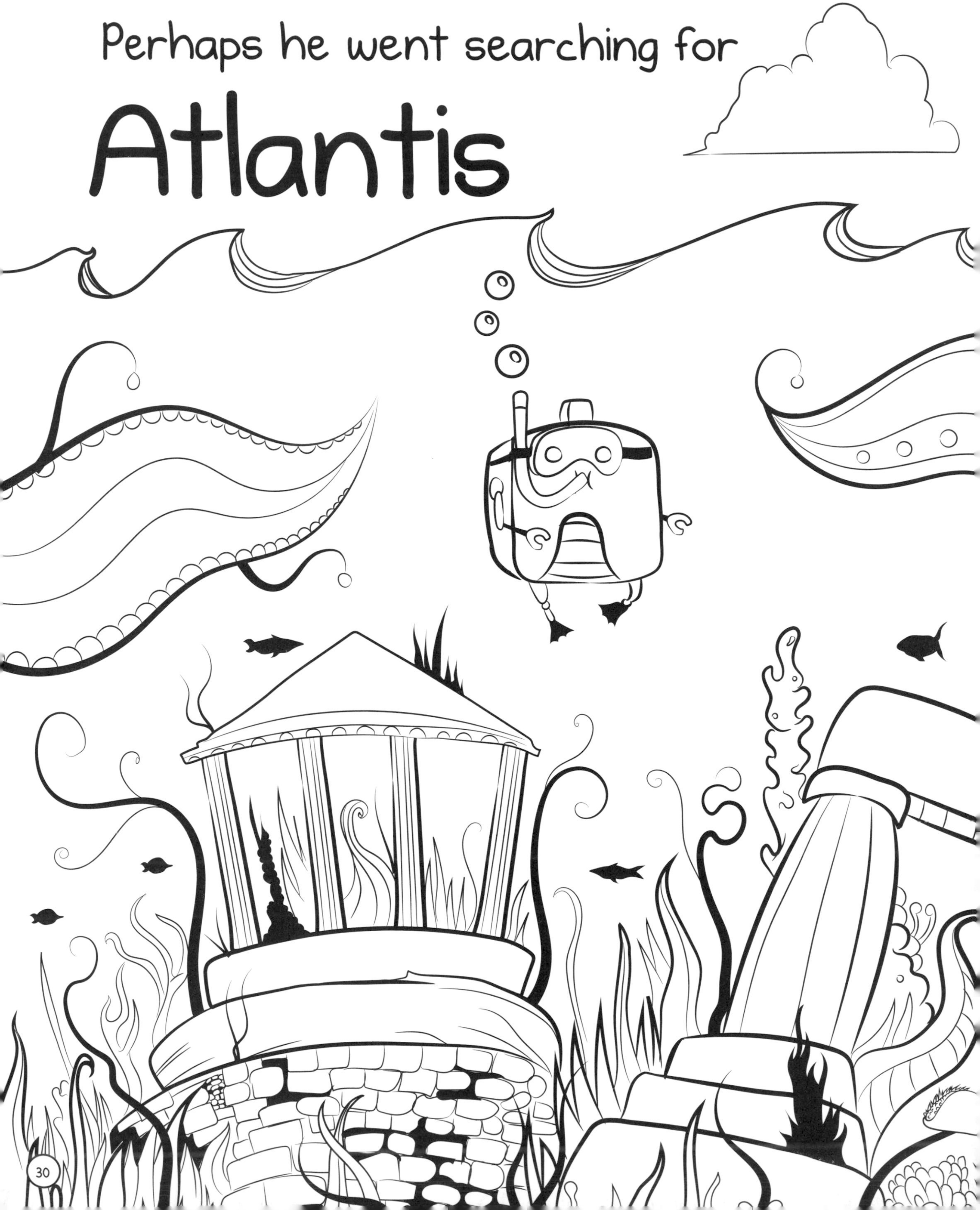

and was attacked by the shrimp we call

mantis.

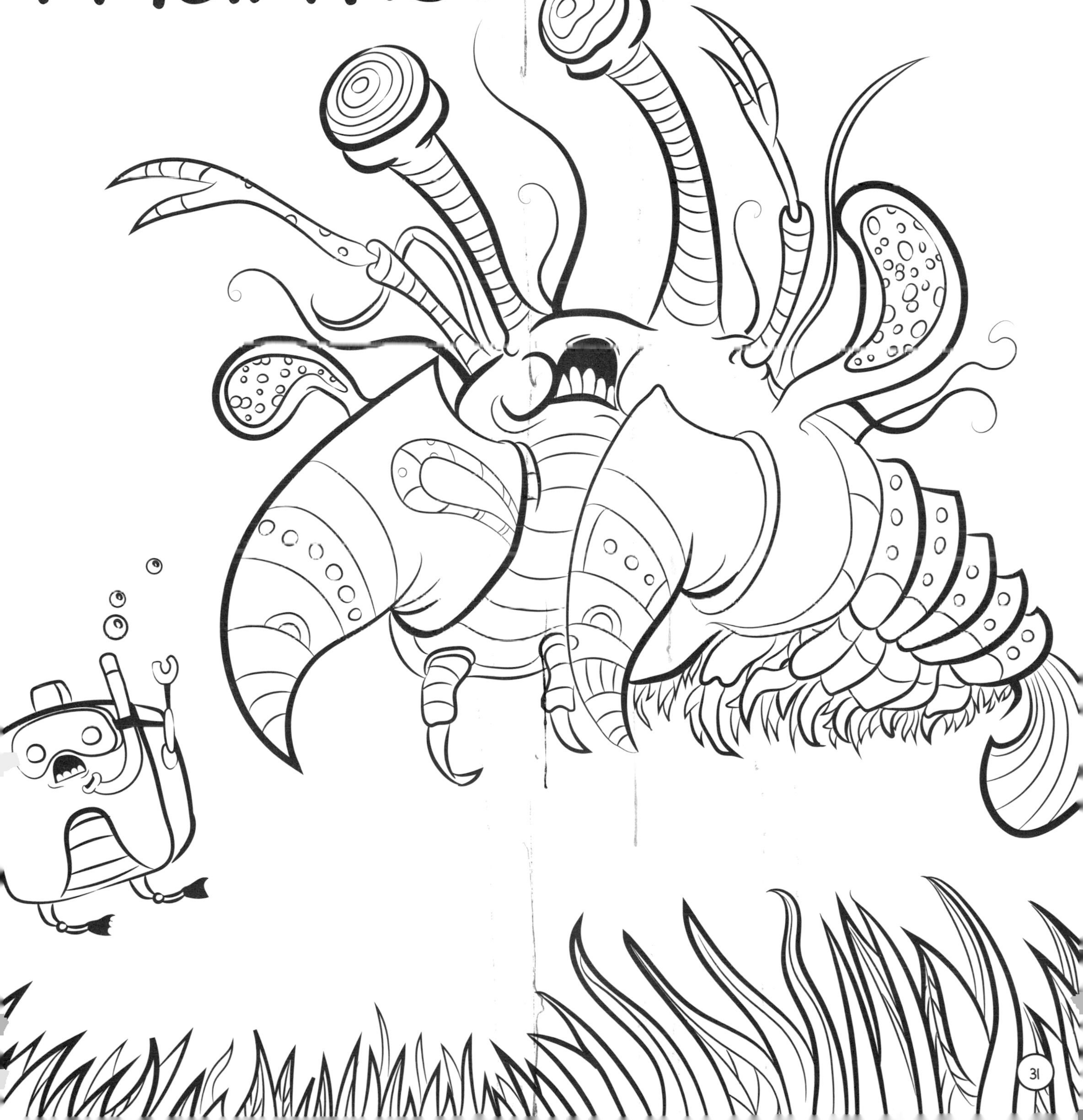

Maybe he spoke to some

despondent corn

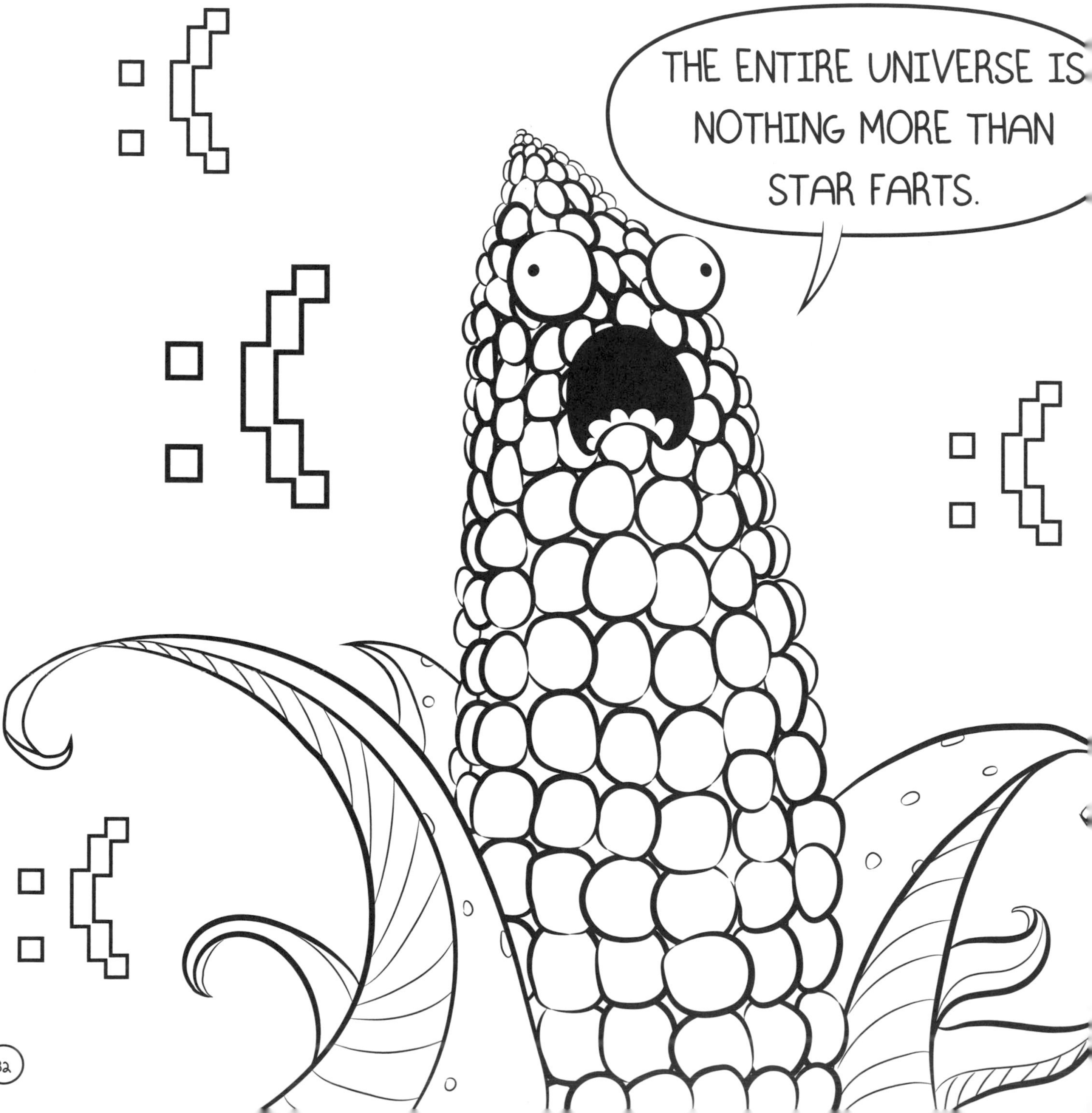
THE ENTIRE UNIVERSE IS NOTHING MORE THAN STAR FARTS.

and he became quite
forlorn.

Or perhaps he spoke to an existential frog

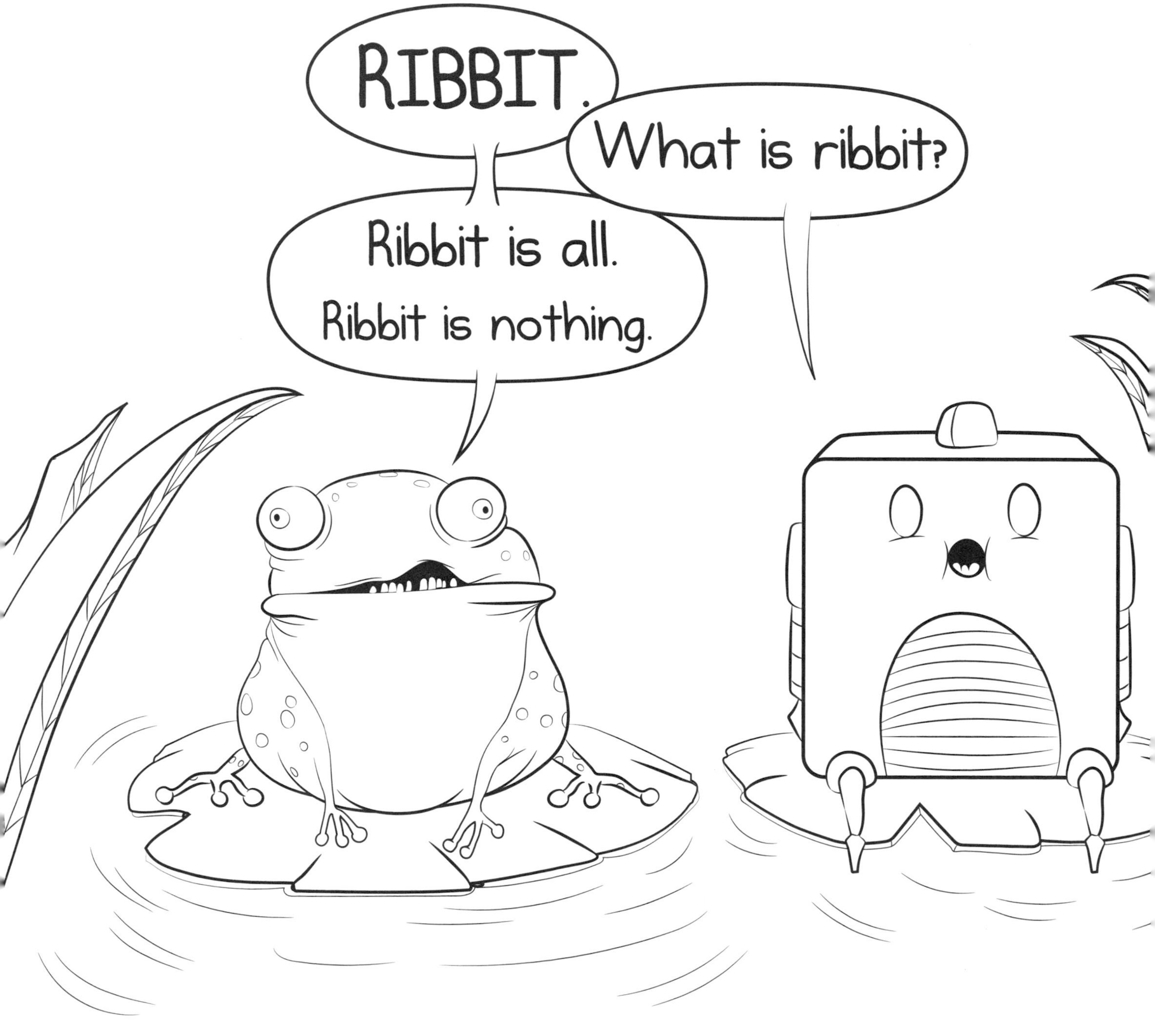

RIBBIT.
What is ribbit?
Ribbit is all.
Ribbit is nothing.

and fell into a

contemplative fog.

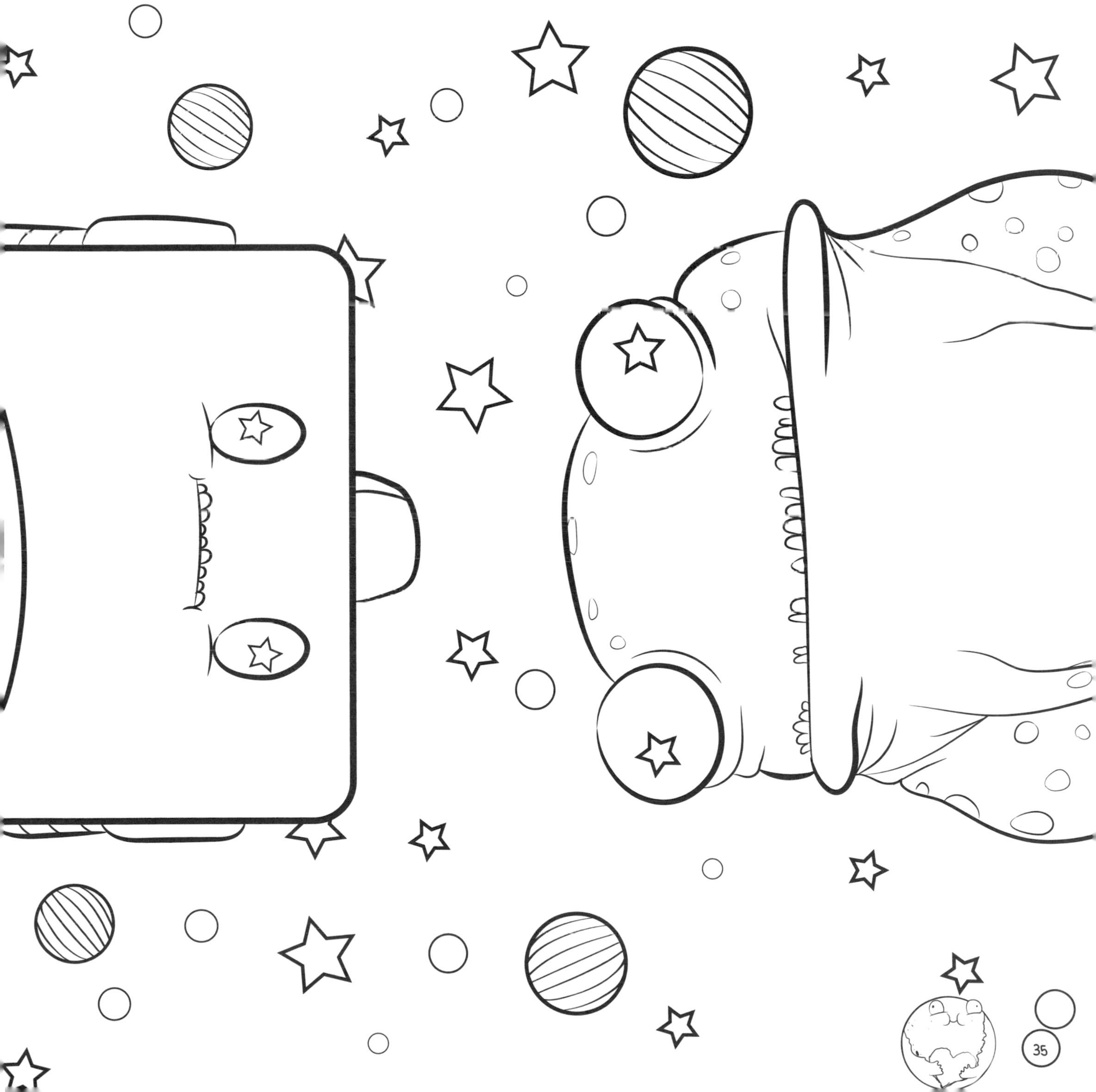

He could have gone to the

chatter holes

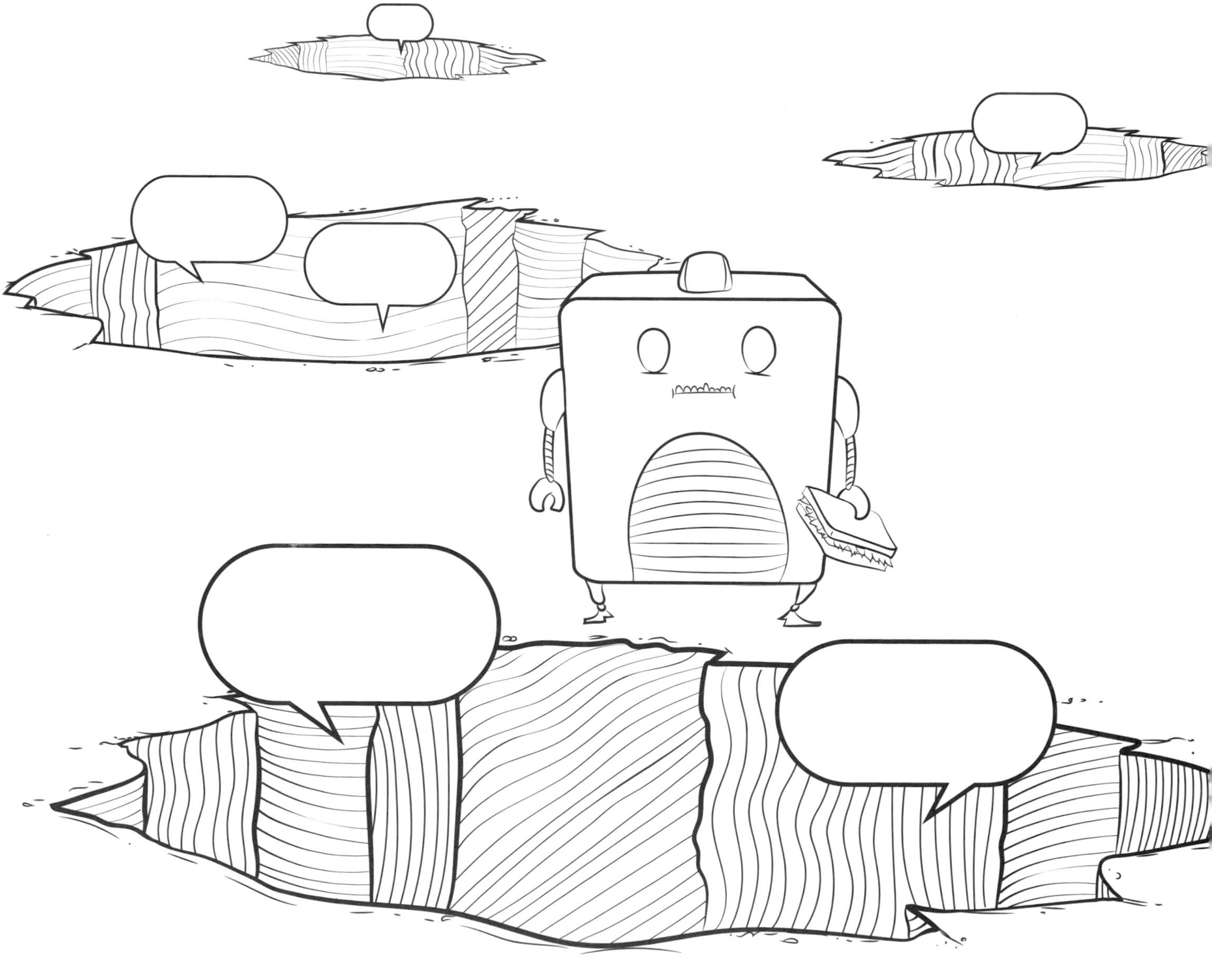

and made the mistake of

feeding the trolls.

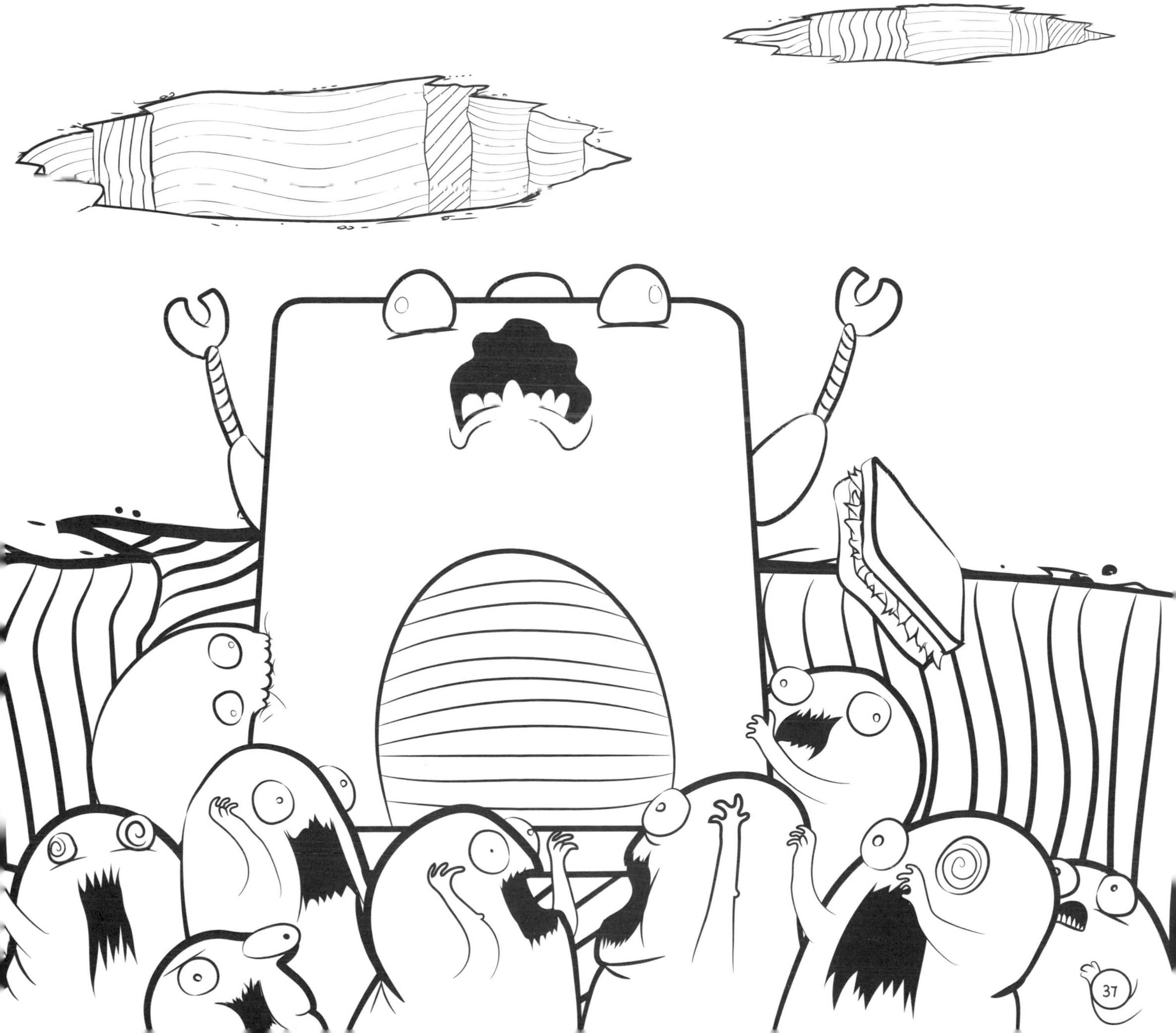

Maybe he chose to

disembark

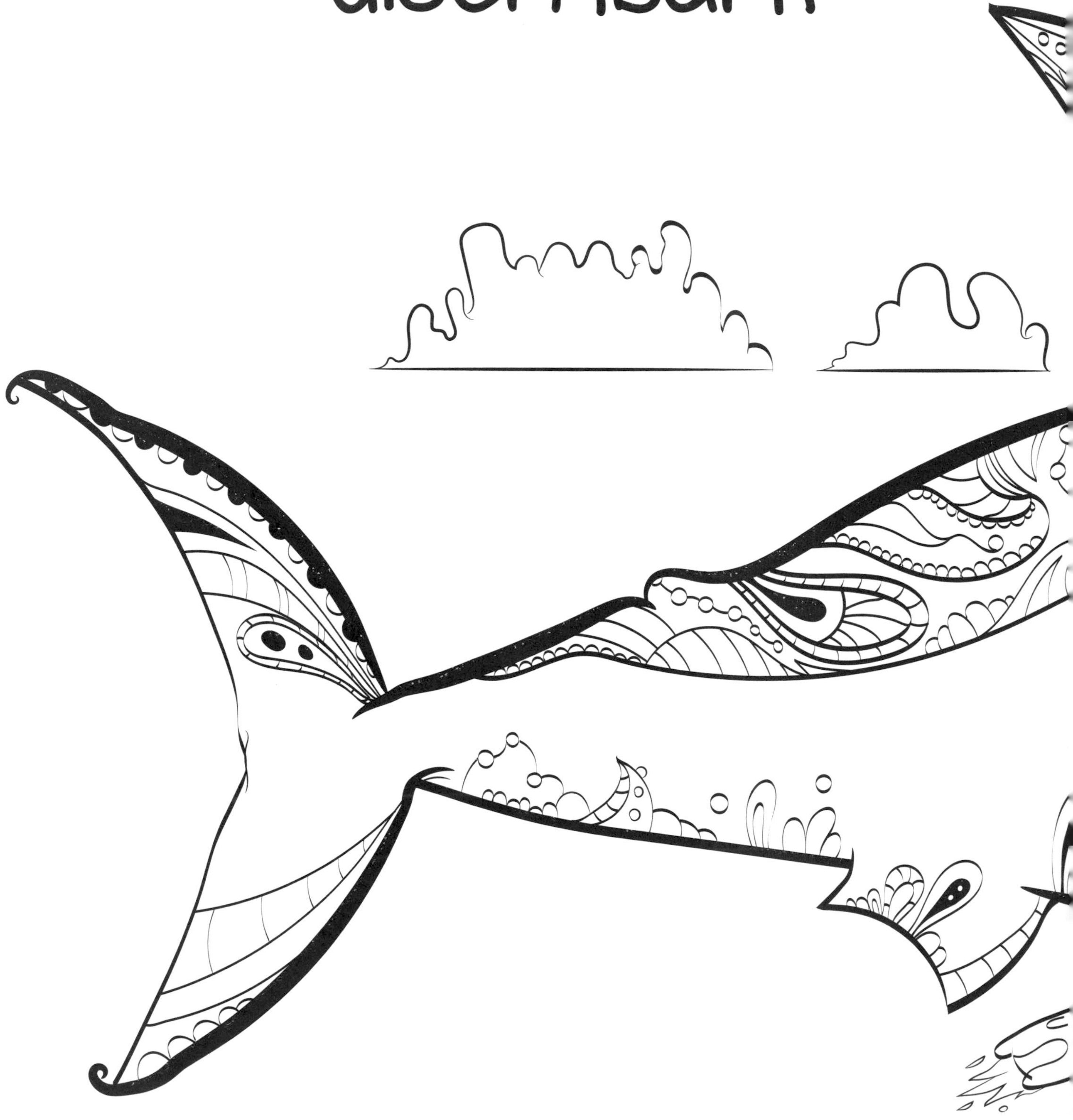

on an airborne

great white shark.

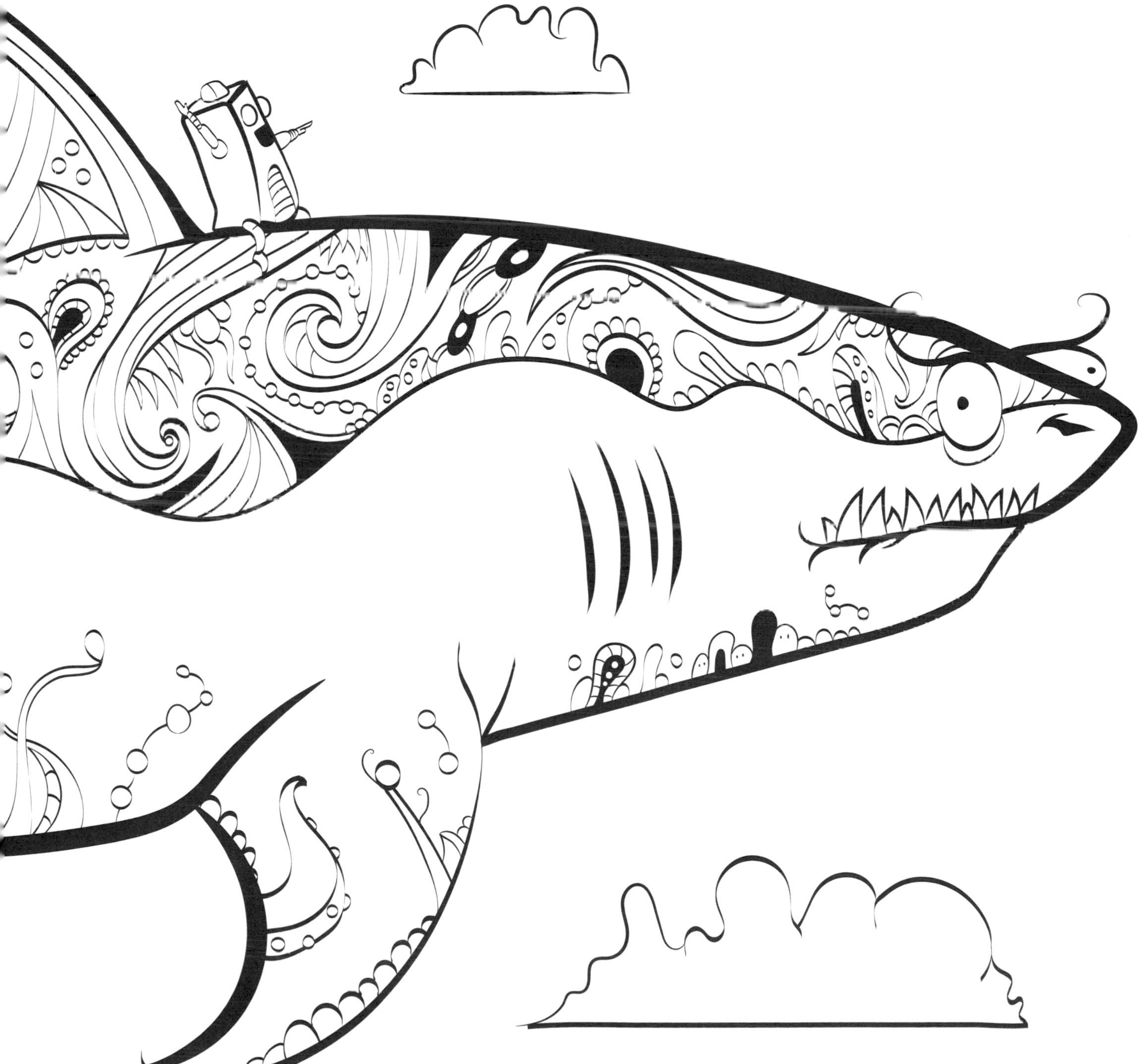

Maybe he had a

battle

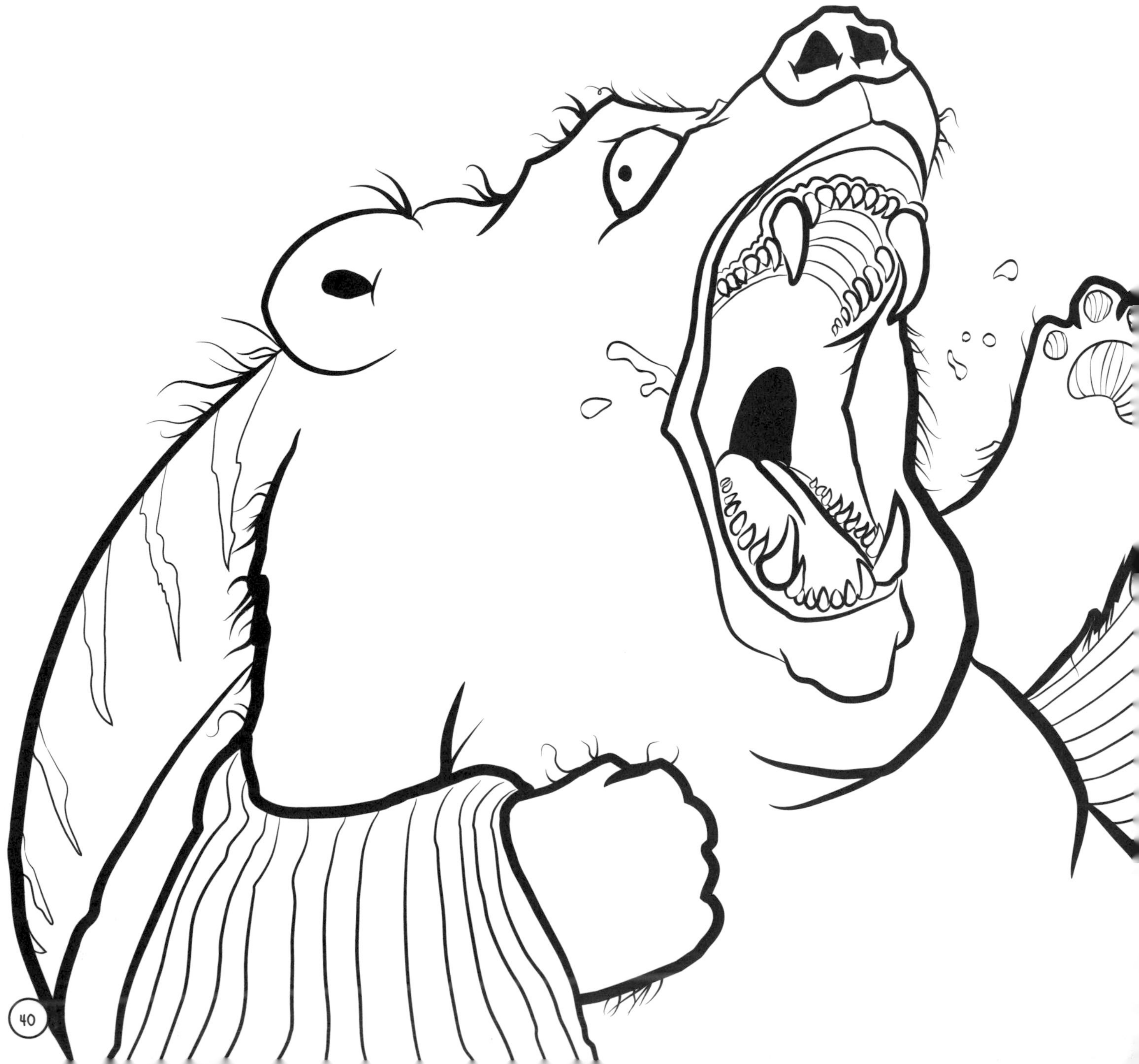

with a fearsome

bear-o-dactyl.

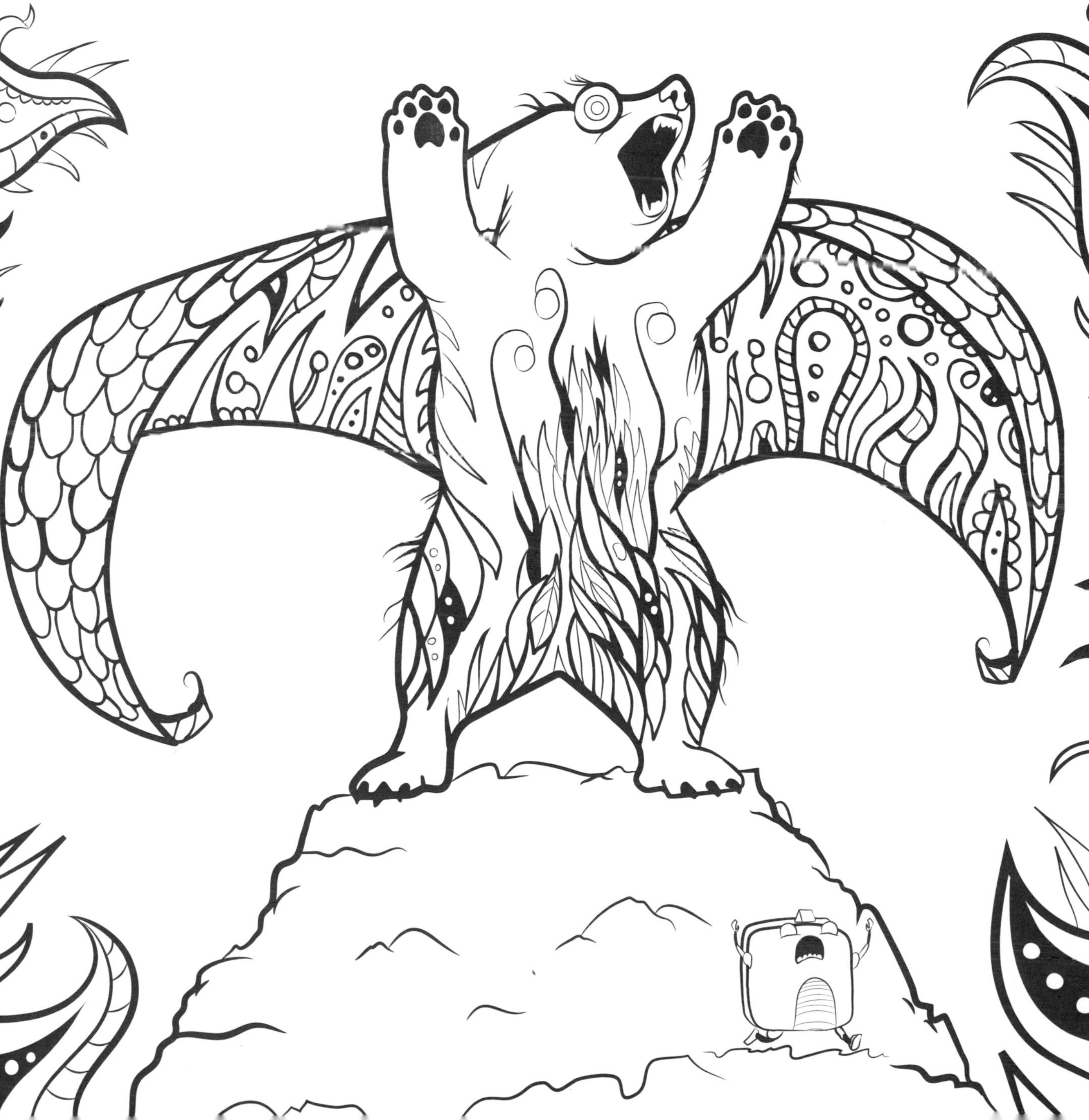

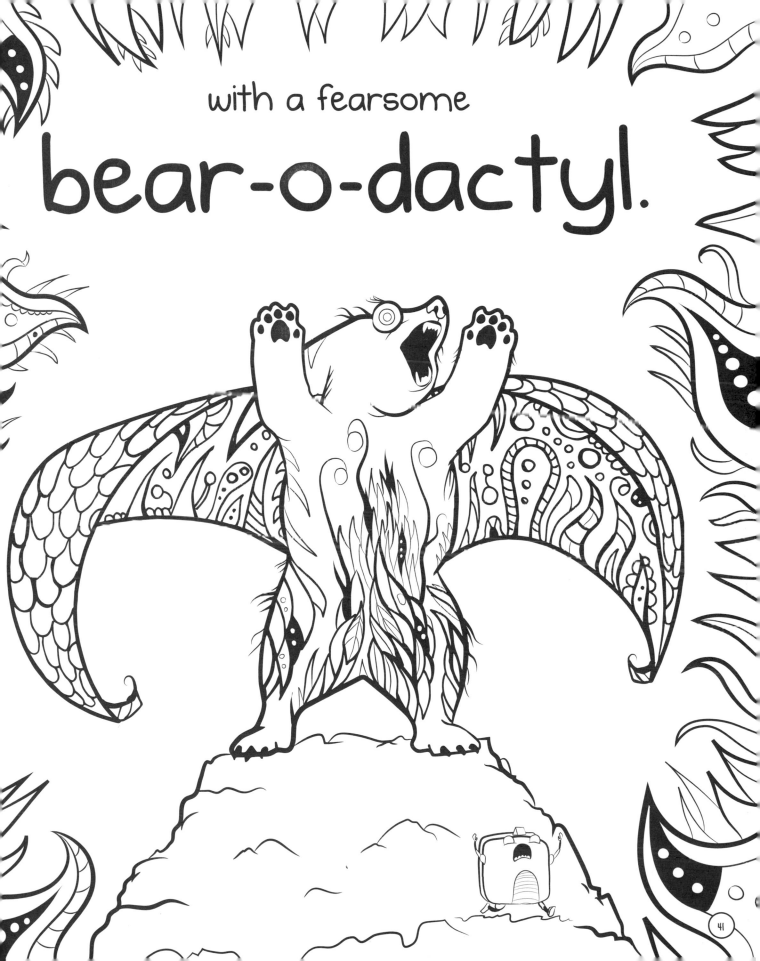

Or perhaps he went

golfin'

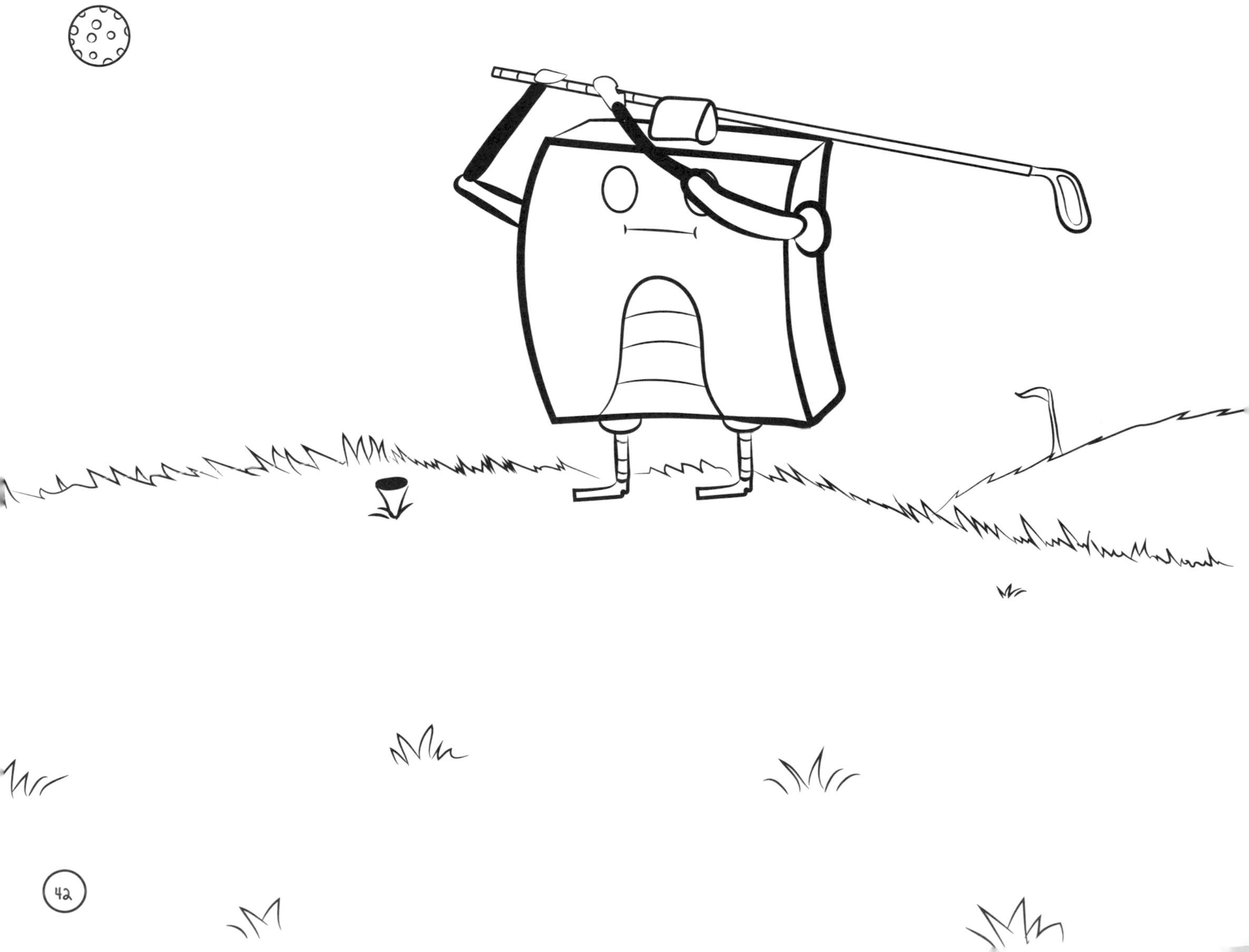

with a pregnant

dolphin.

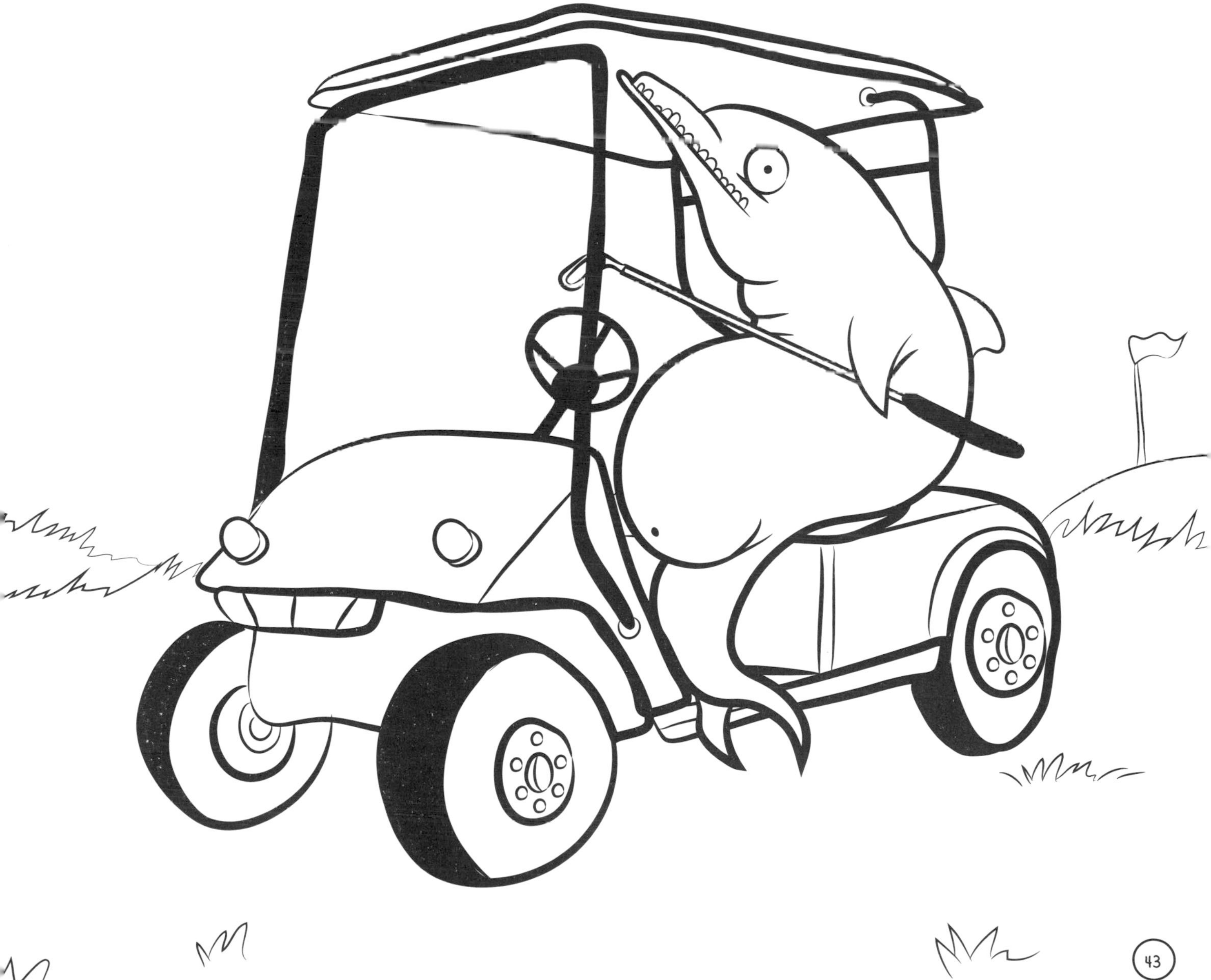

Or maybe he got a

smackin'

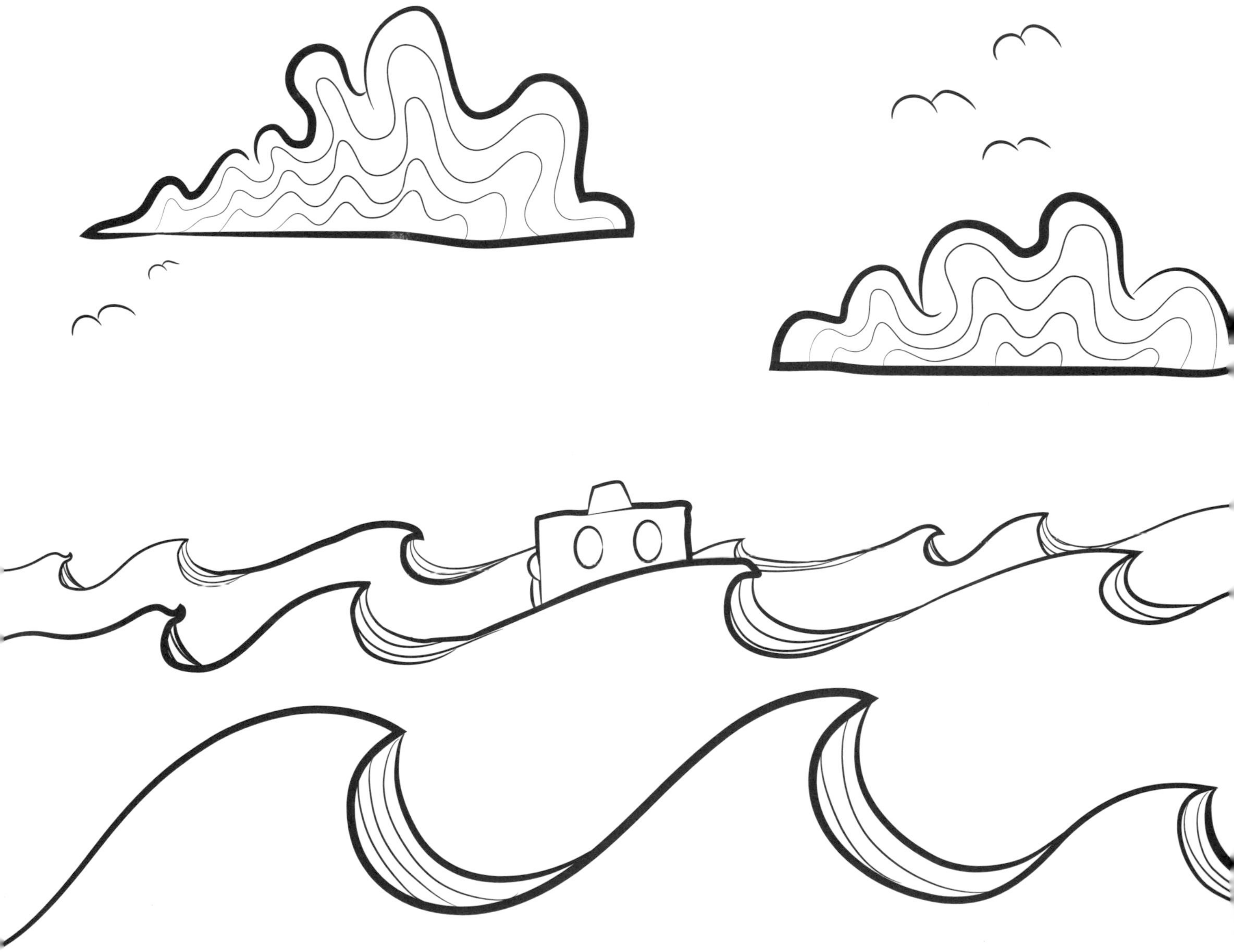

from an angry

kraken.

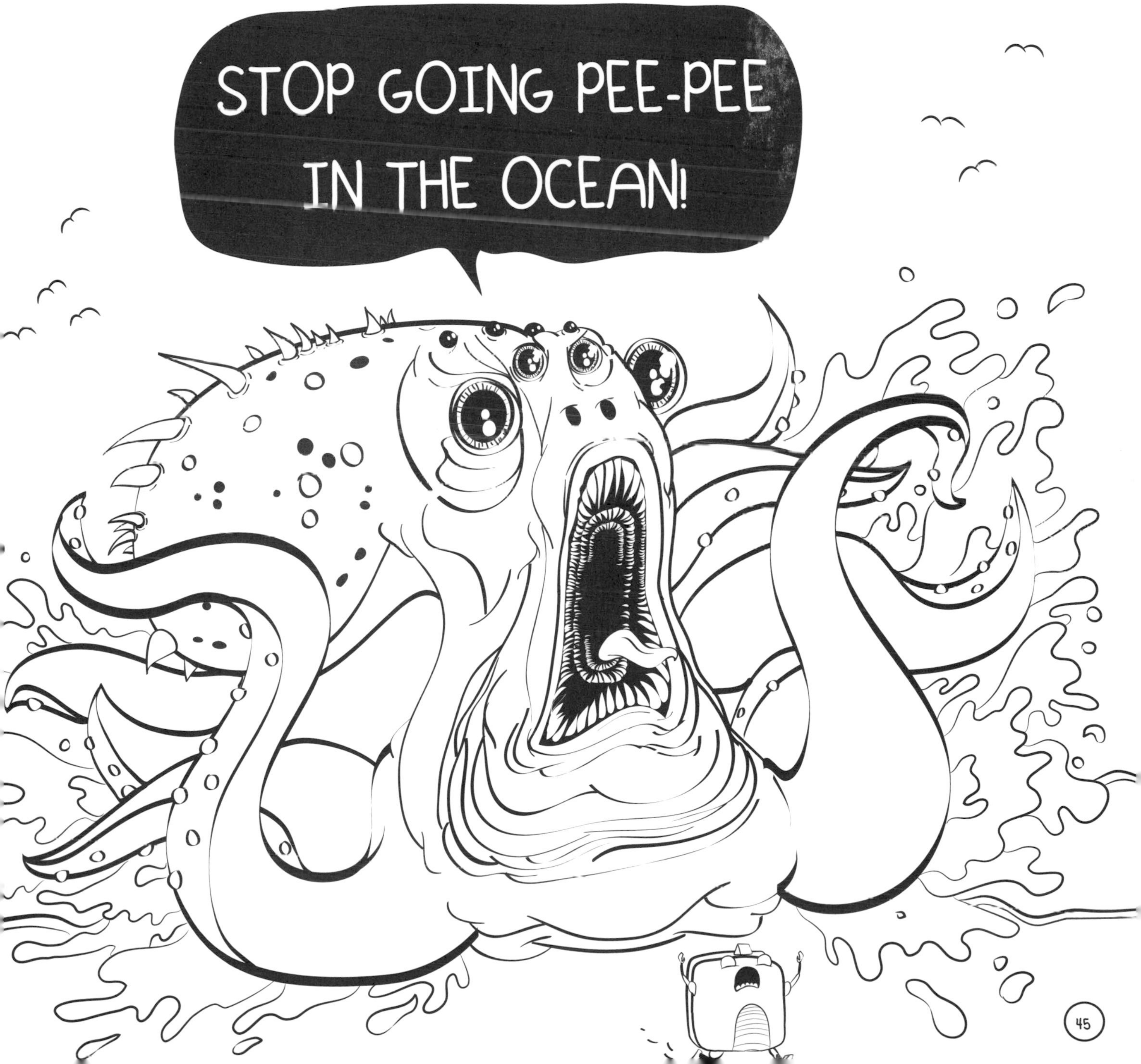
STOP GOING PEE-PEE
IN THE OCEAN!

Maybe he met a pair of
baby owls,

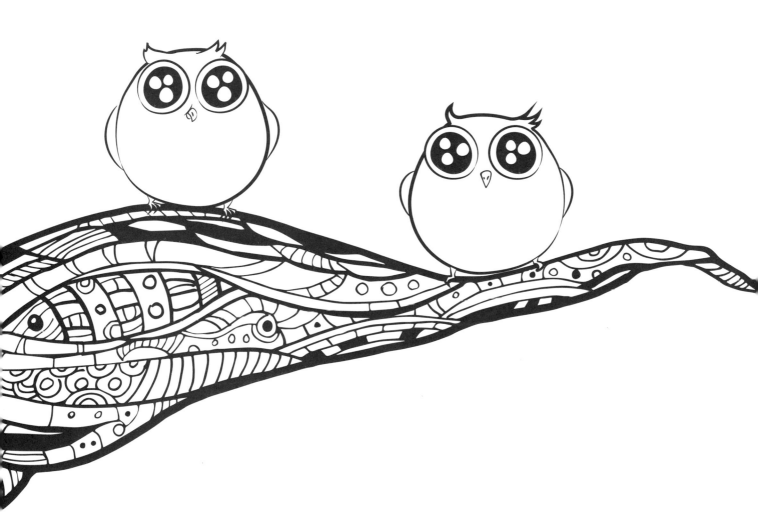

and they became the

best of pals.

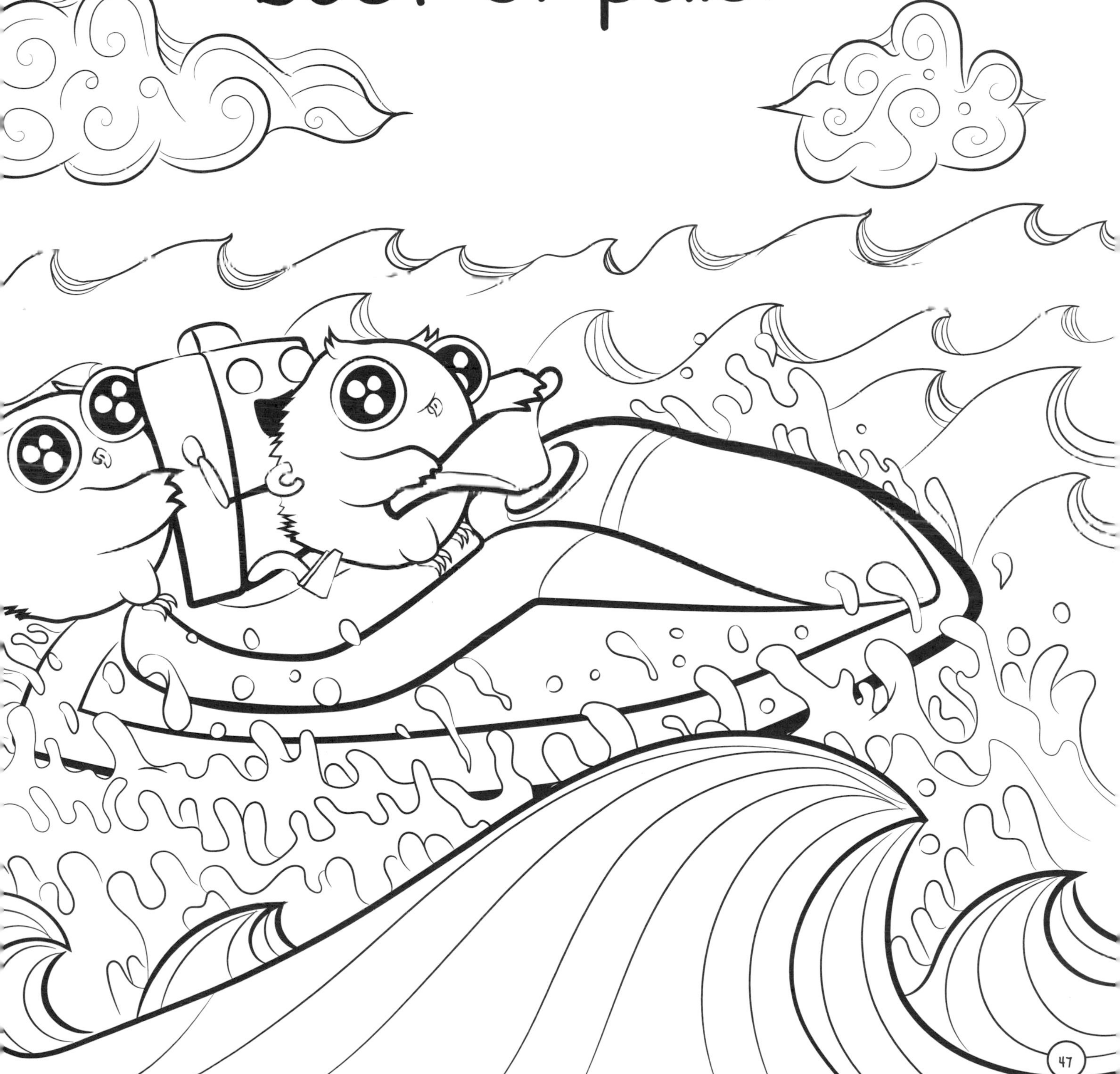

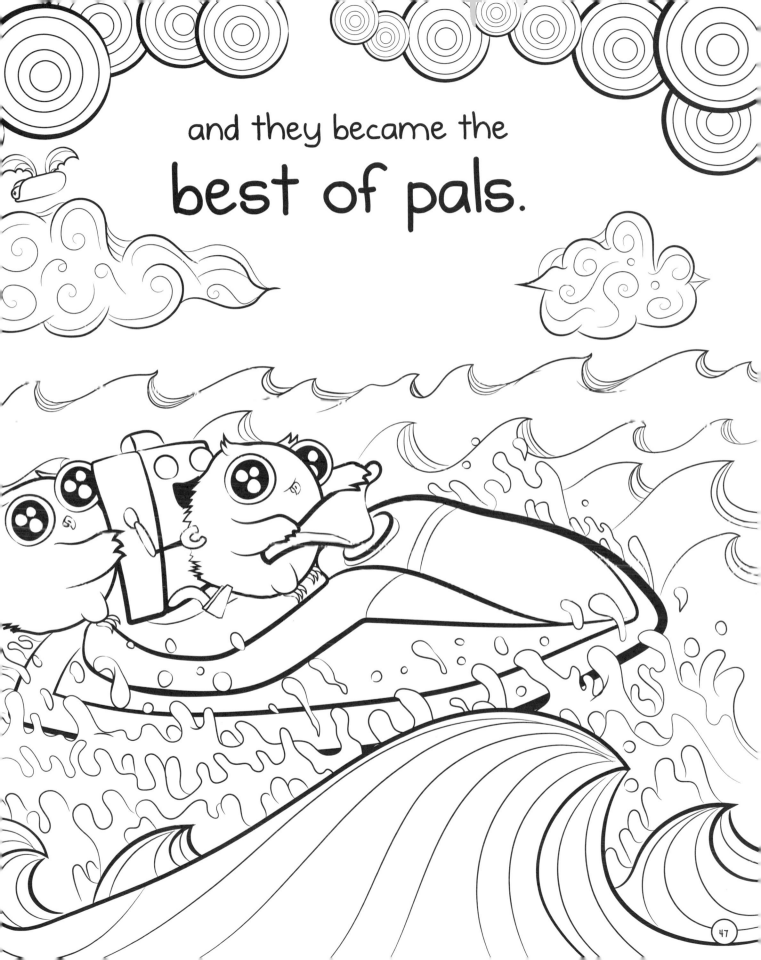

Maybe they started playing with

knives

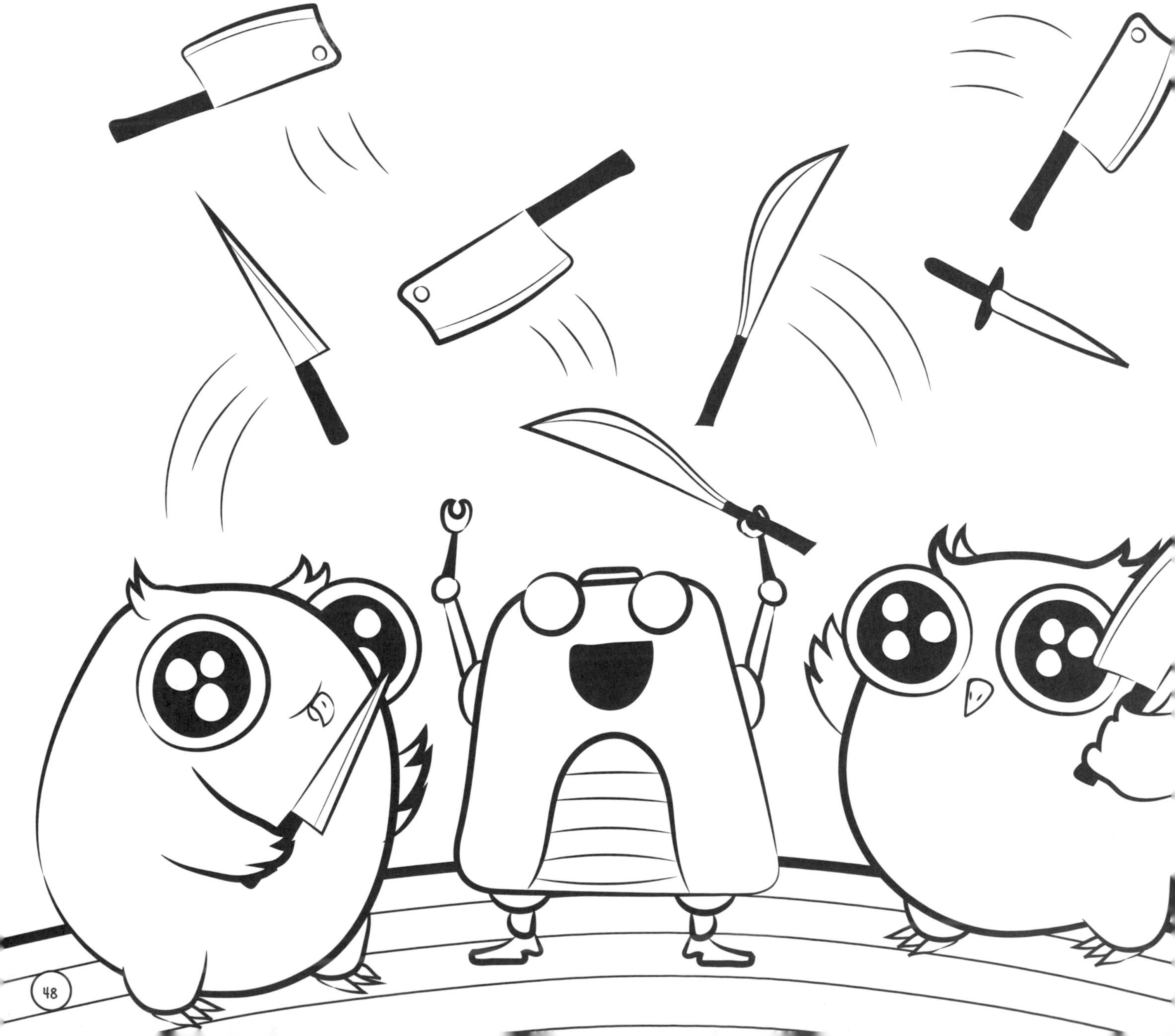

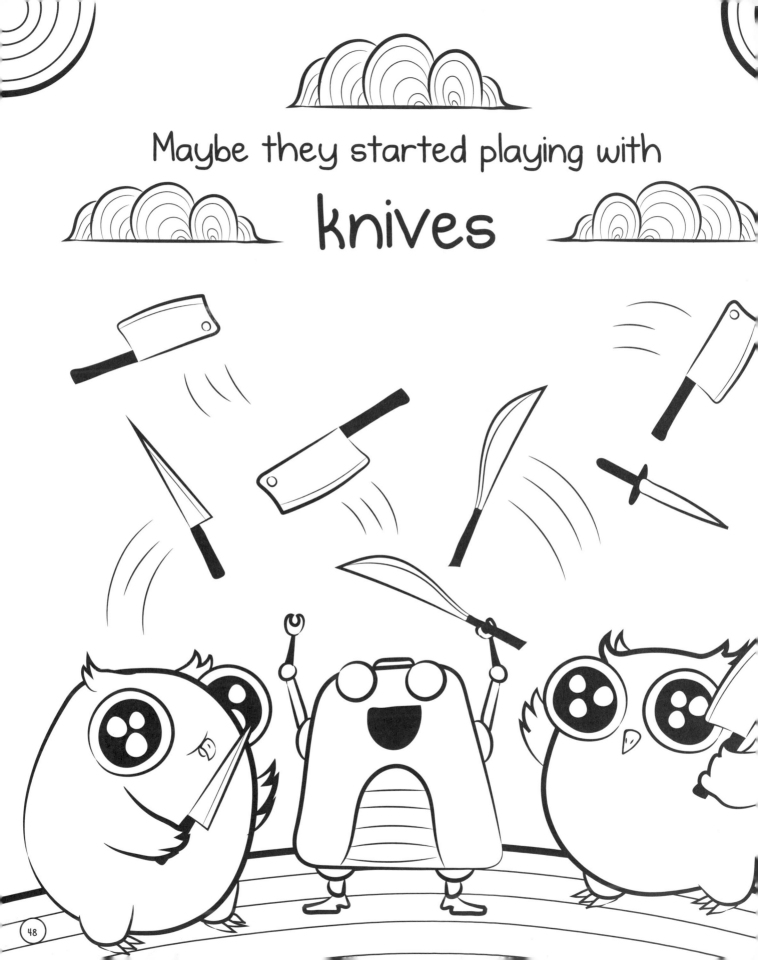

while giving each other SWEET

high fives.

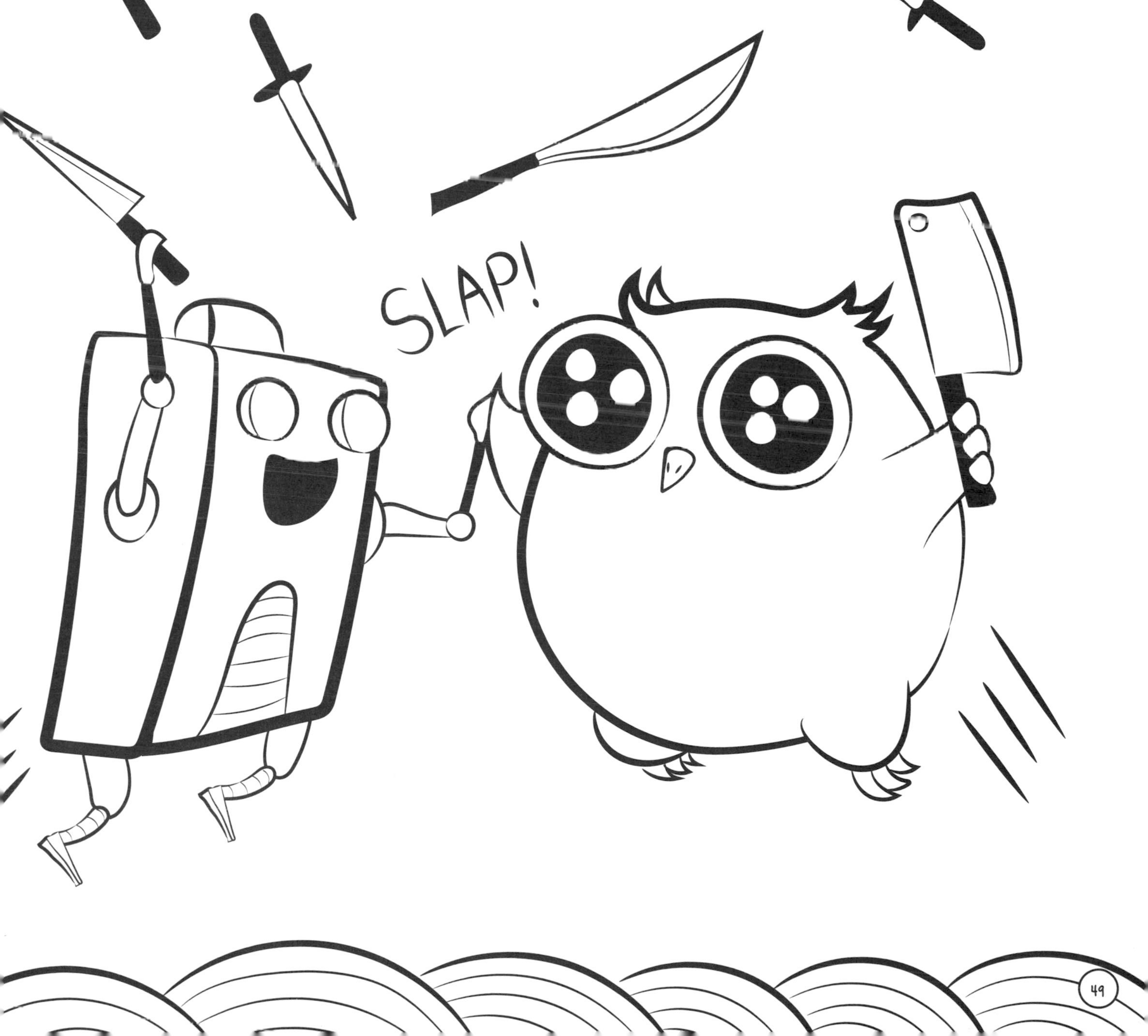
SLAP!

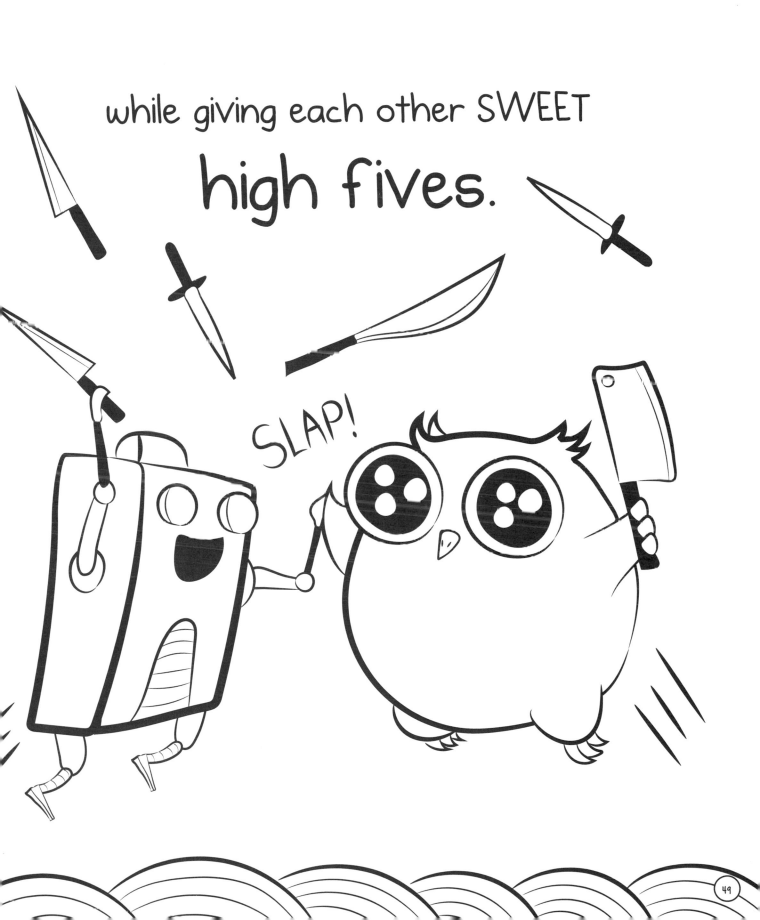

And maybe on those knives,

he slipped and fell,

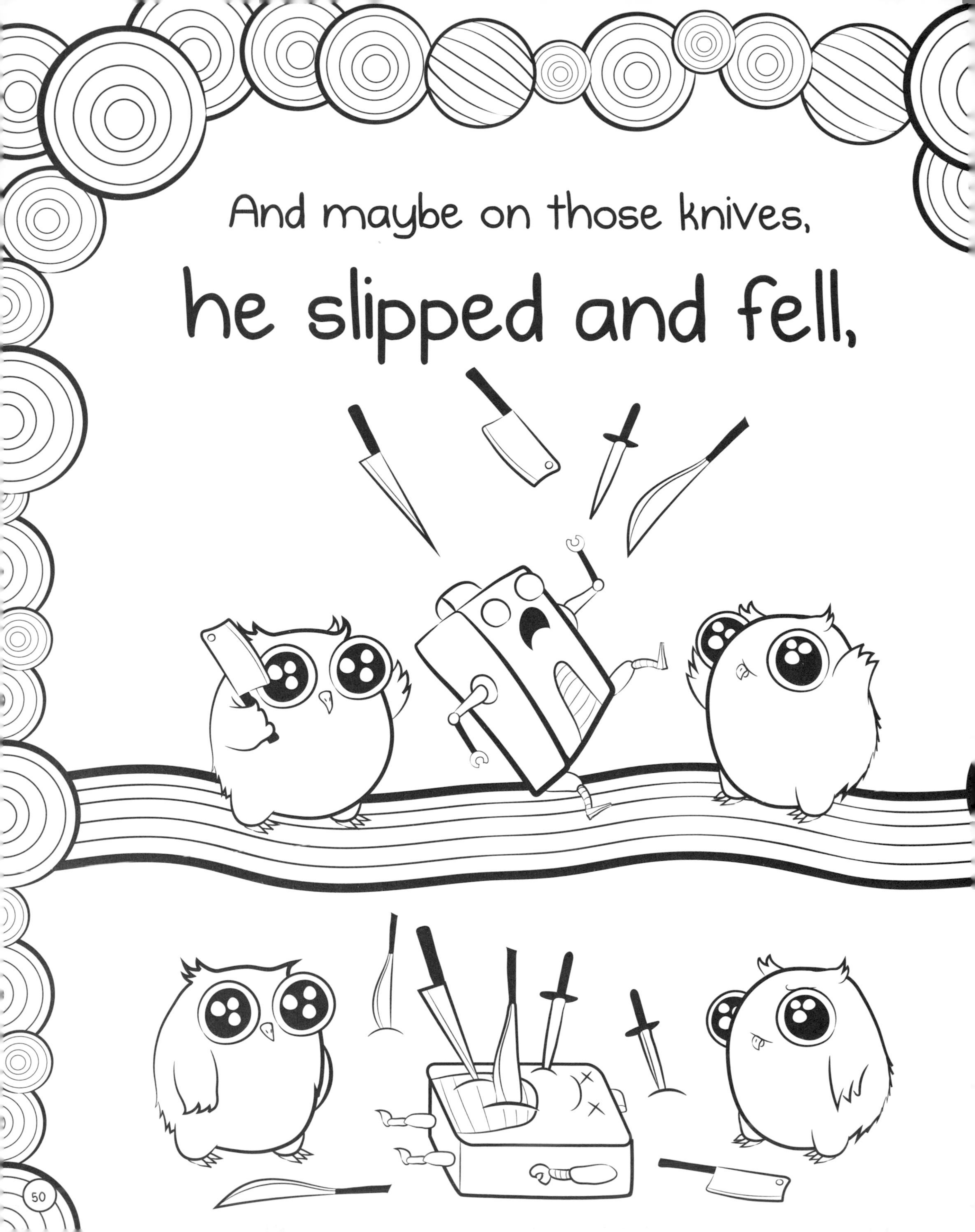

so they buried his body,

and buried it well.

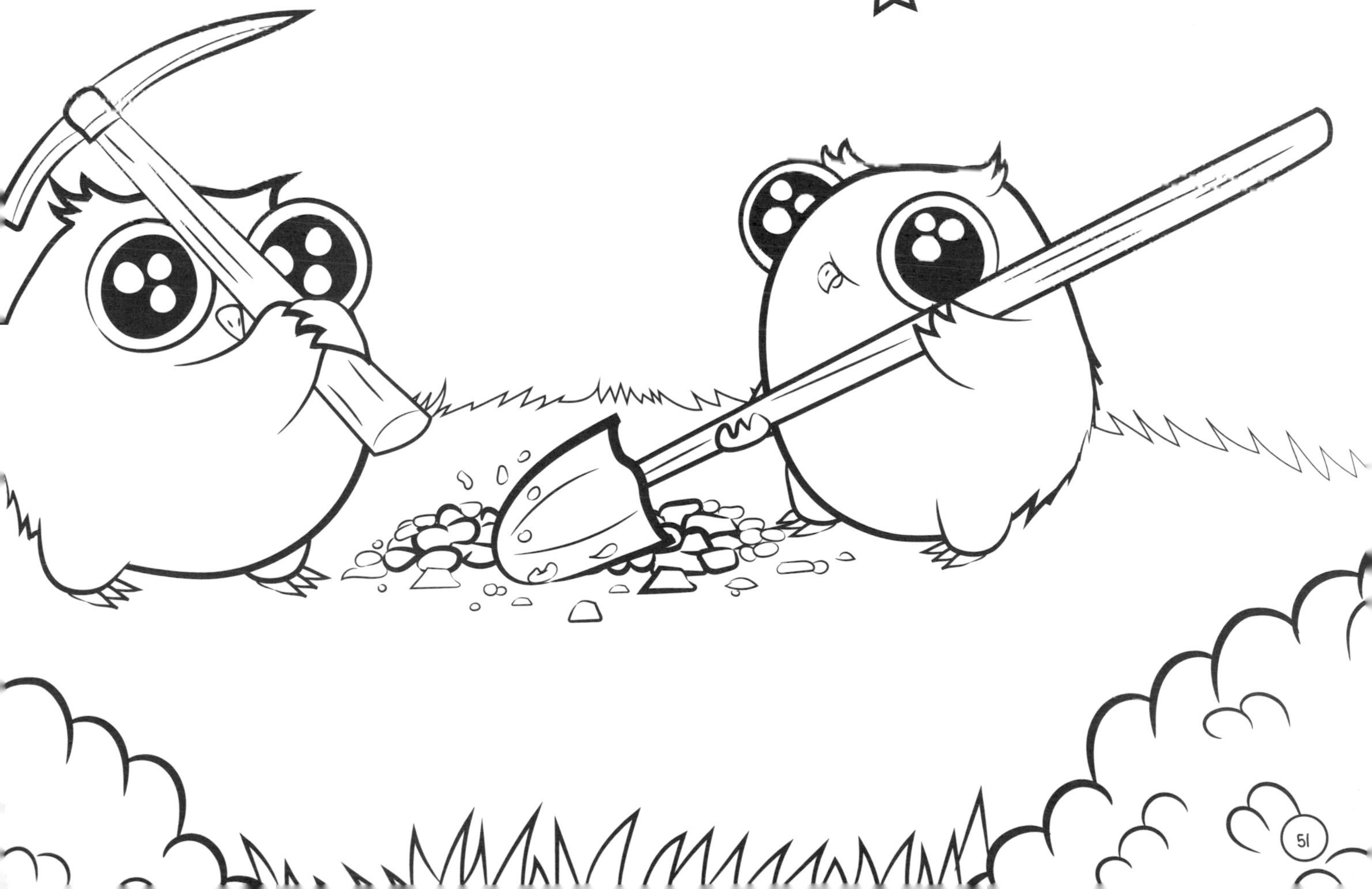

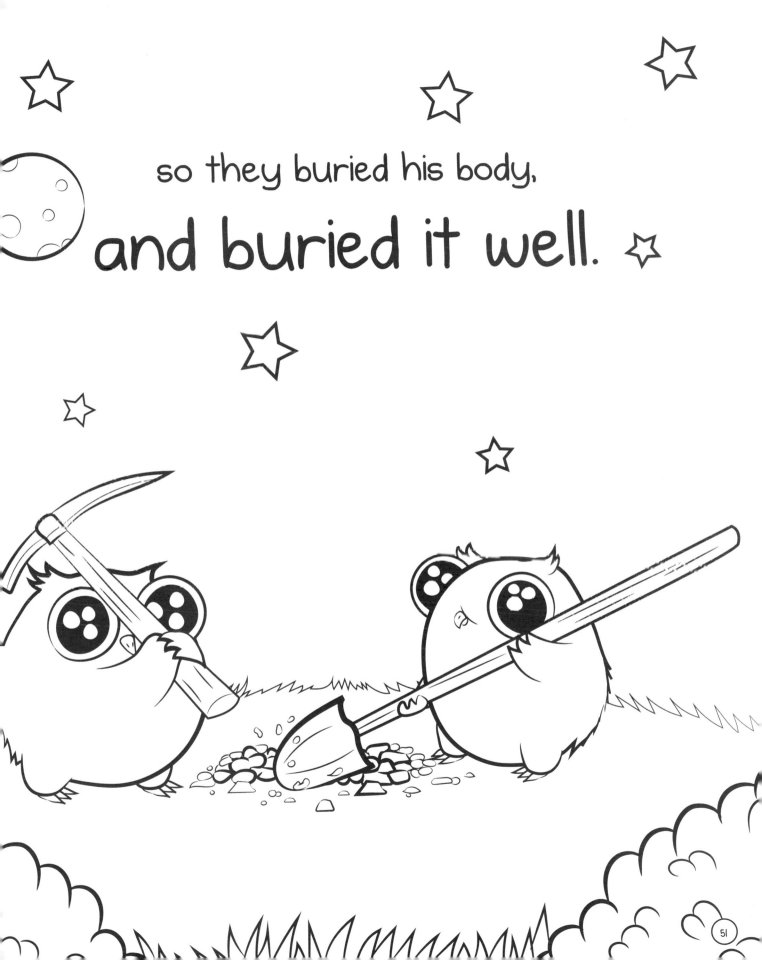

Perhaps he hung with some

party bats,

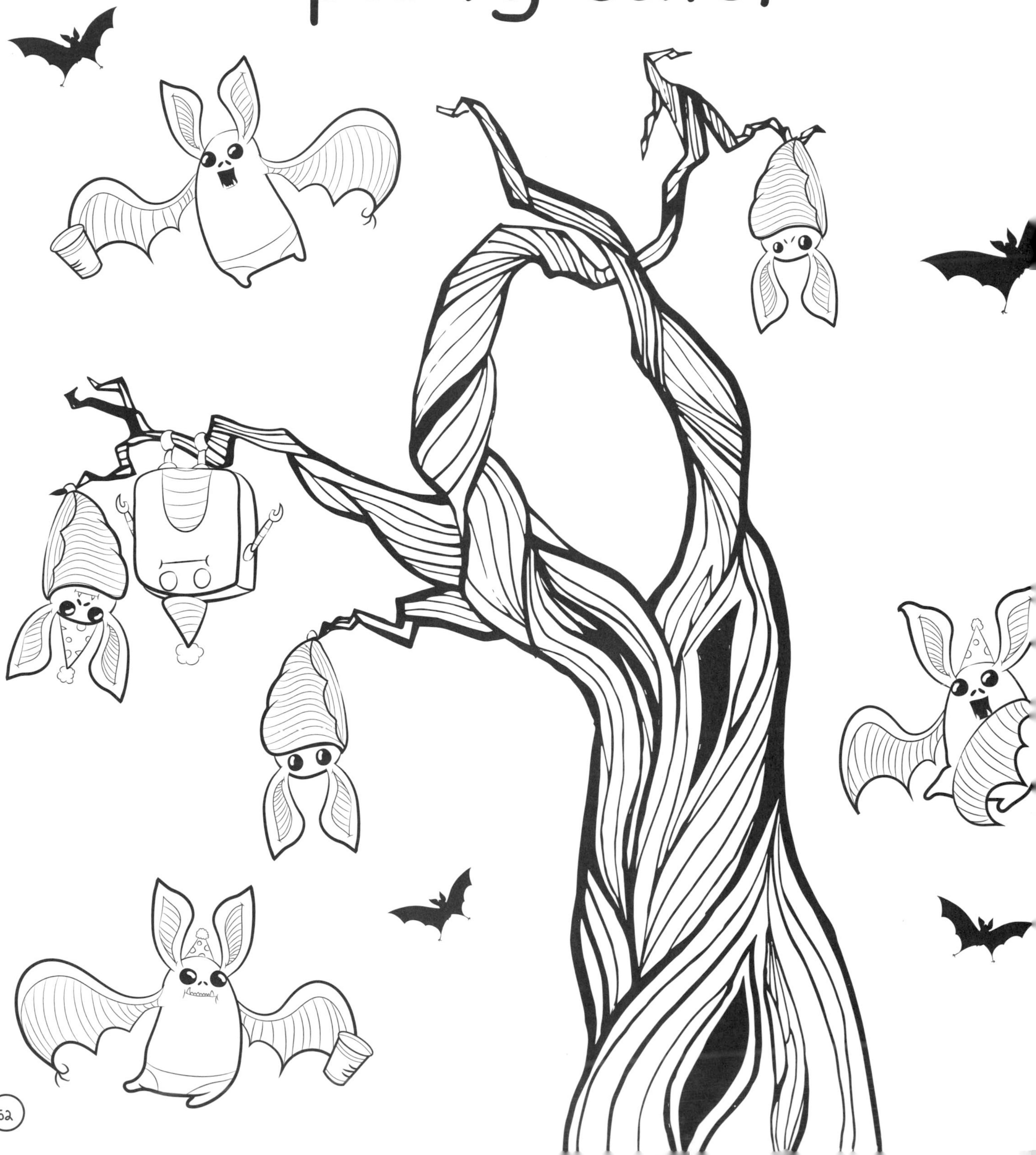

and of their party juice,

he drank an

entire vat.

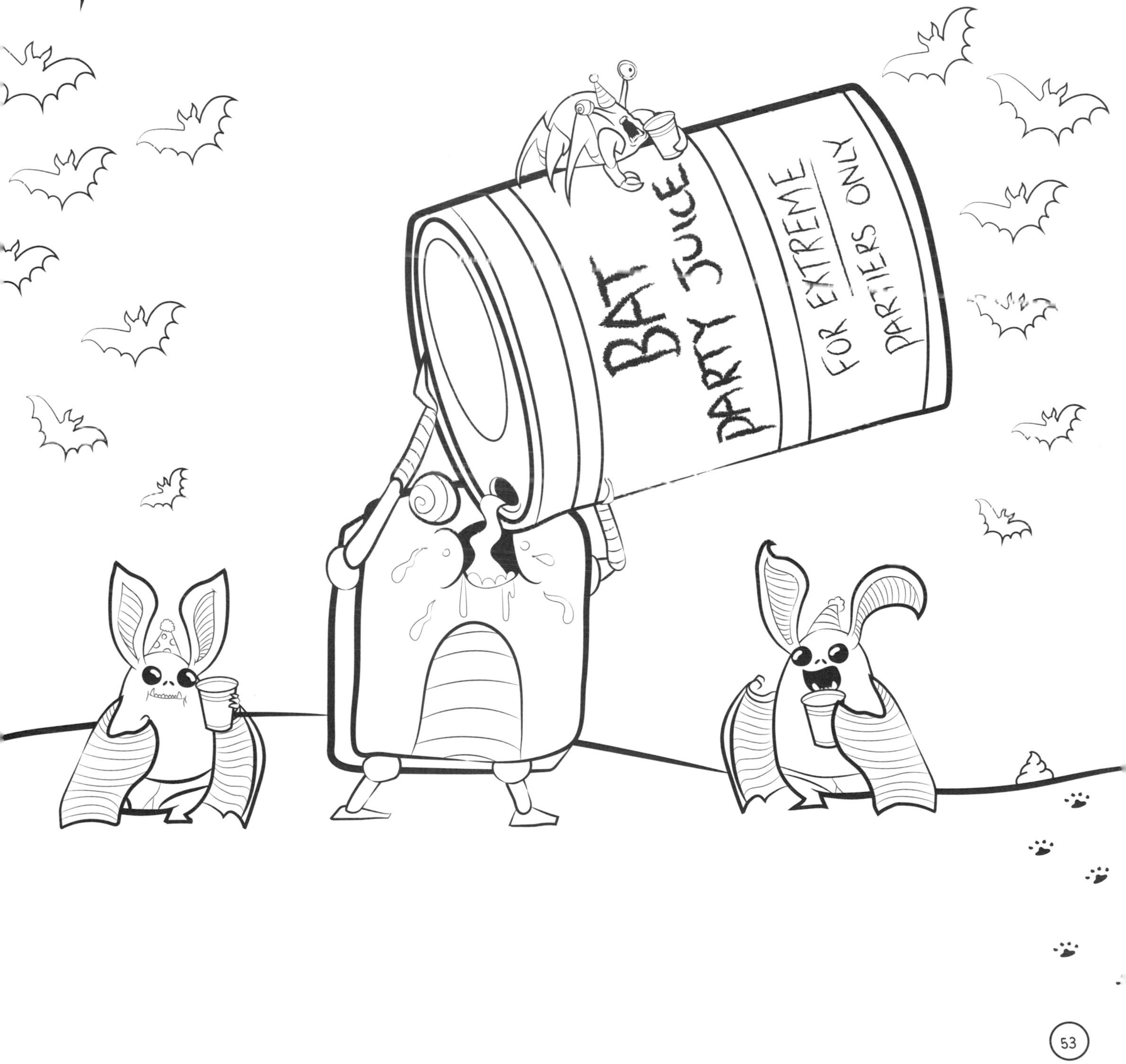

BAT PARTY JUICE
FOR EXTREME PARTIERS ONLY

This was **way** too much,

so he

retched and hurled,

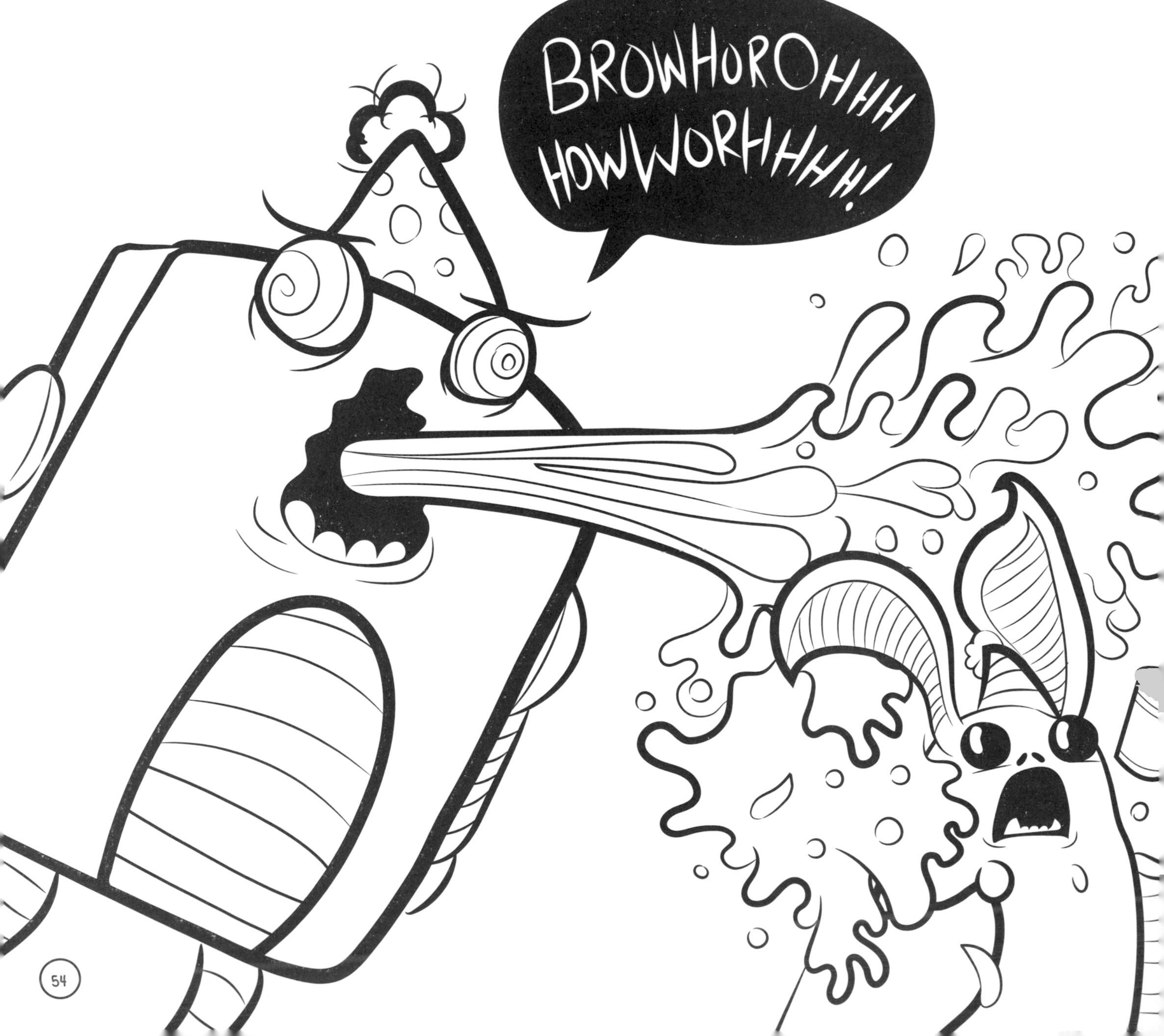
BROWHOROHHHH
HOWWORHHHHH!

and his

robot barf

filled up the

world.

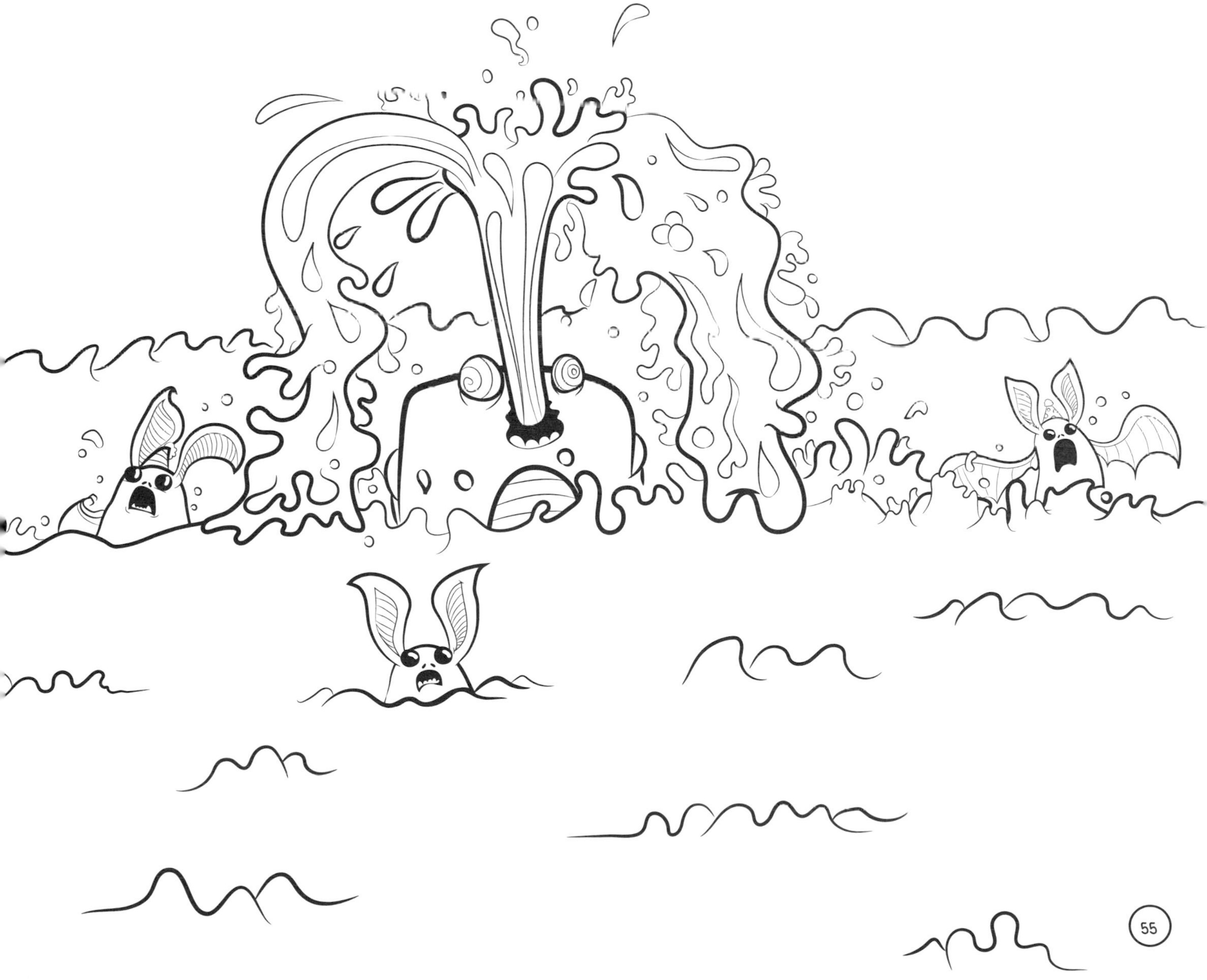

Perhaps he isn't lost

at all.

He didn't vanish, die, slip,

or fall.

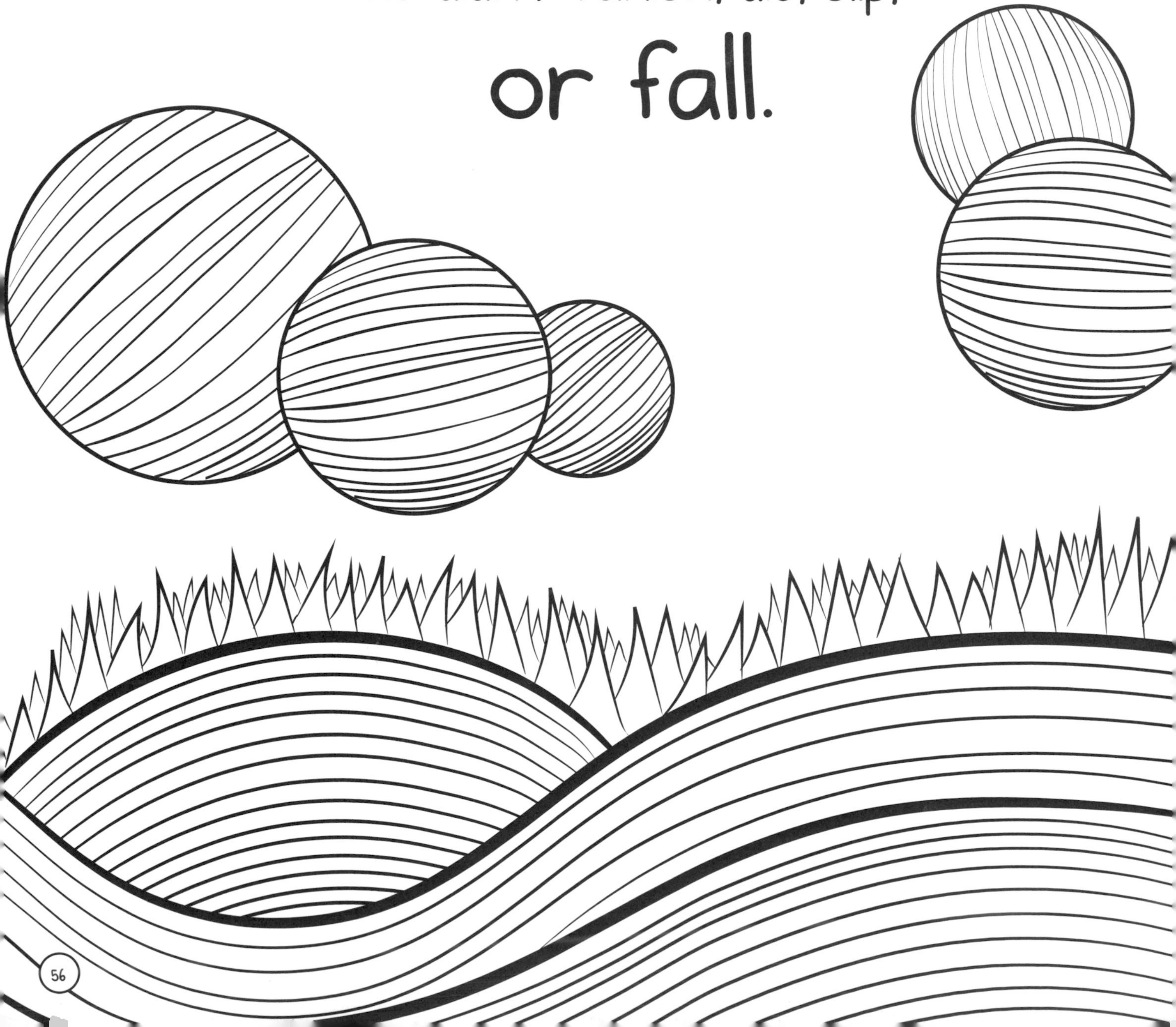

Perhaps, instead,
we'll never know.

And maybe this is a part of
letting go.

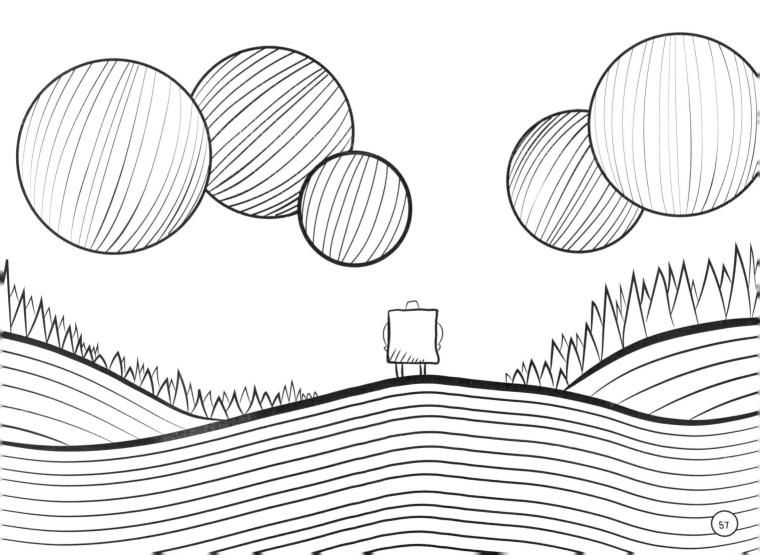

People change,

robots too.

They leave us behind,

when they're through.

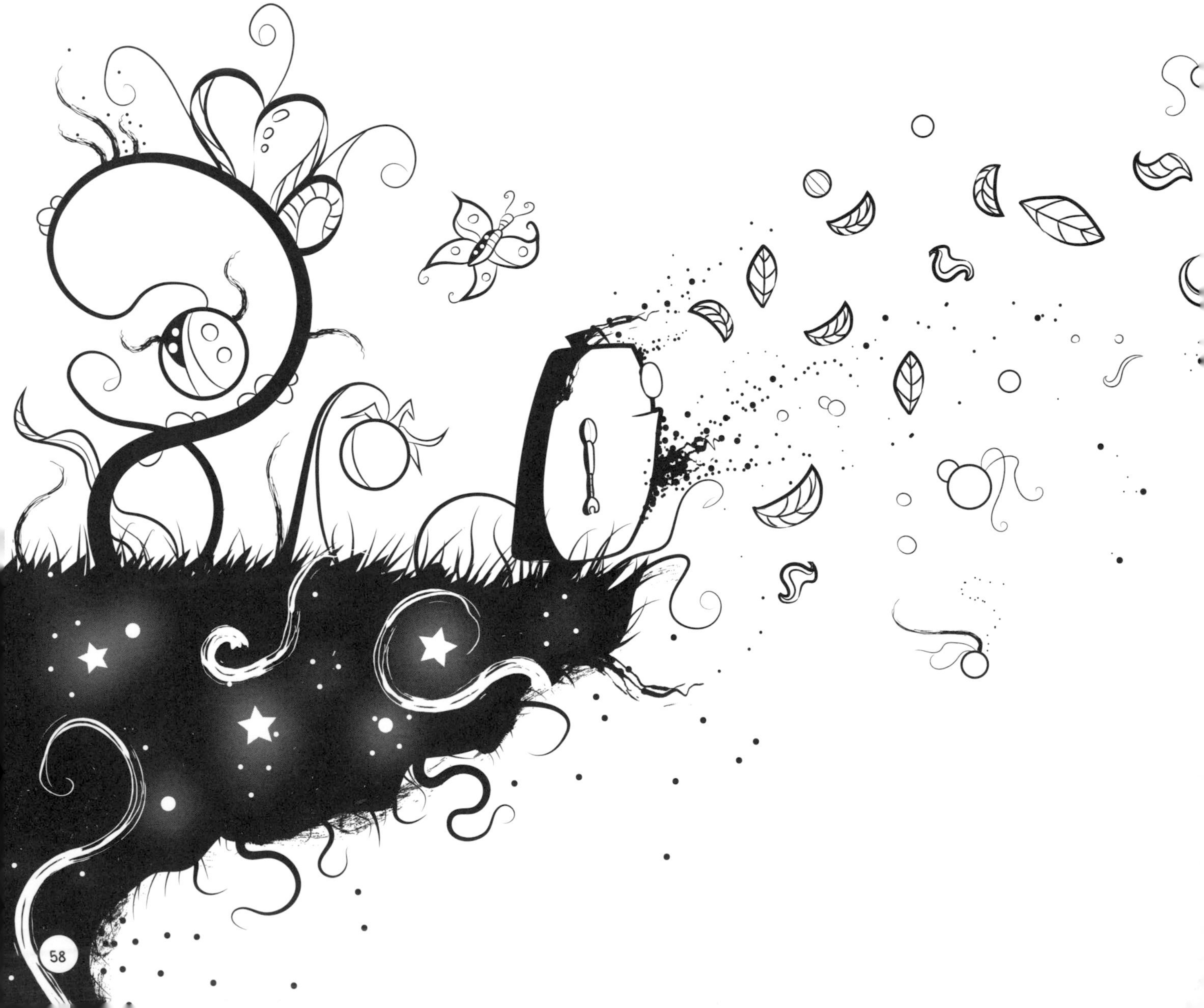

That ending is a bummer!

It's incredibly sad!

Surely something better

could be had.

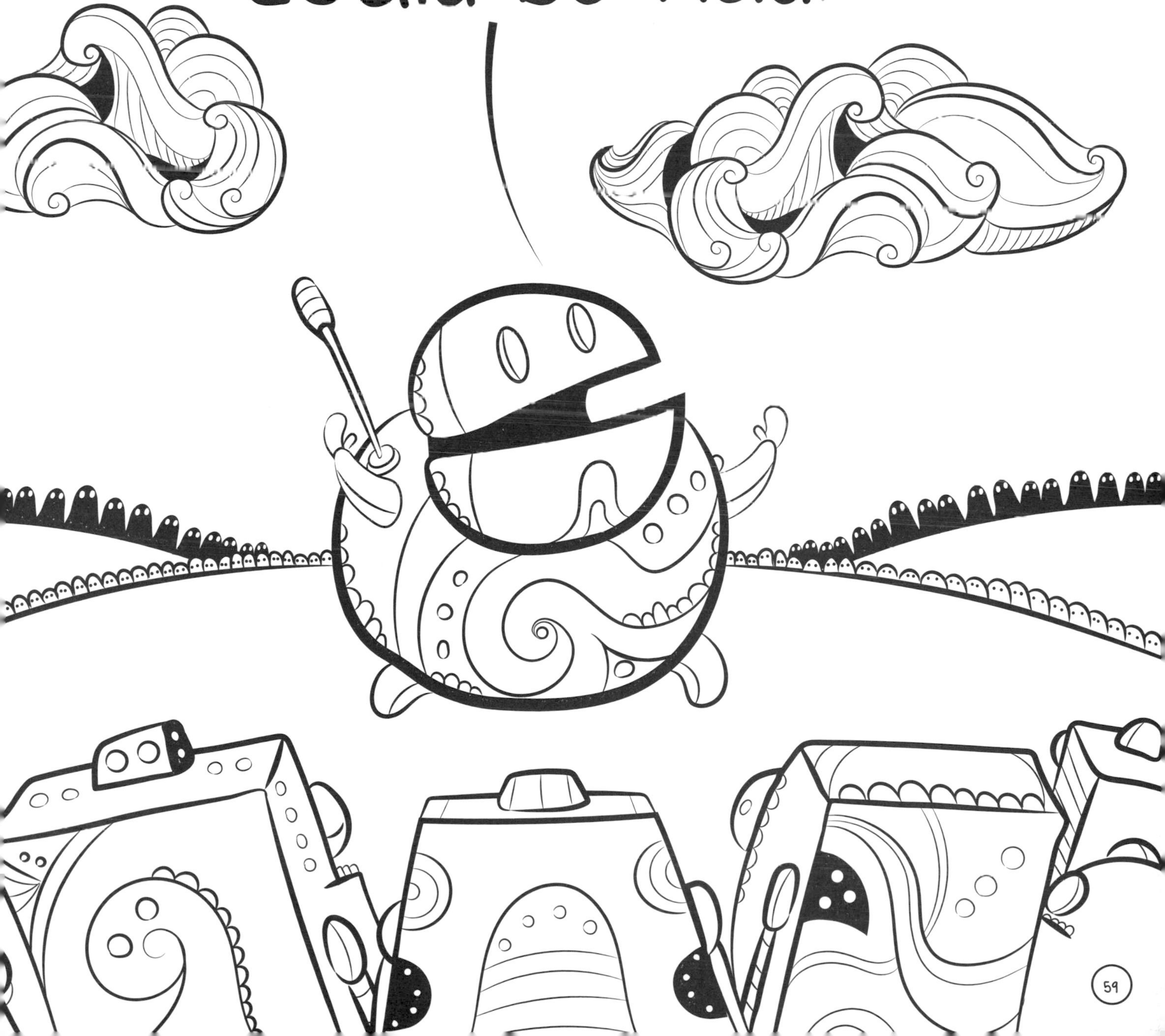

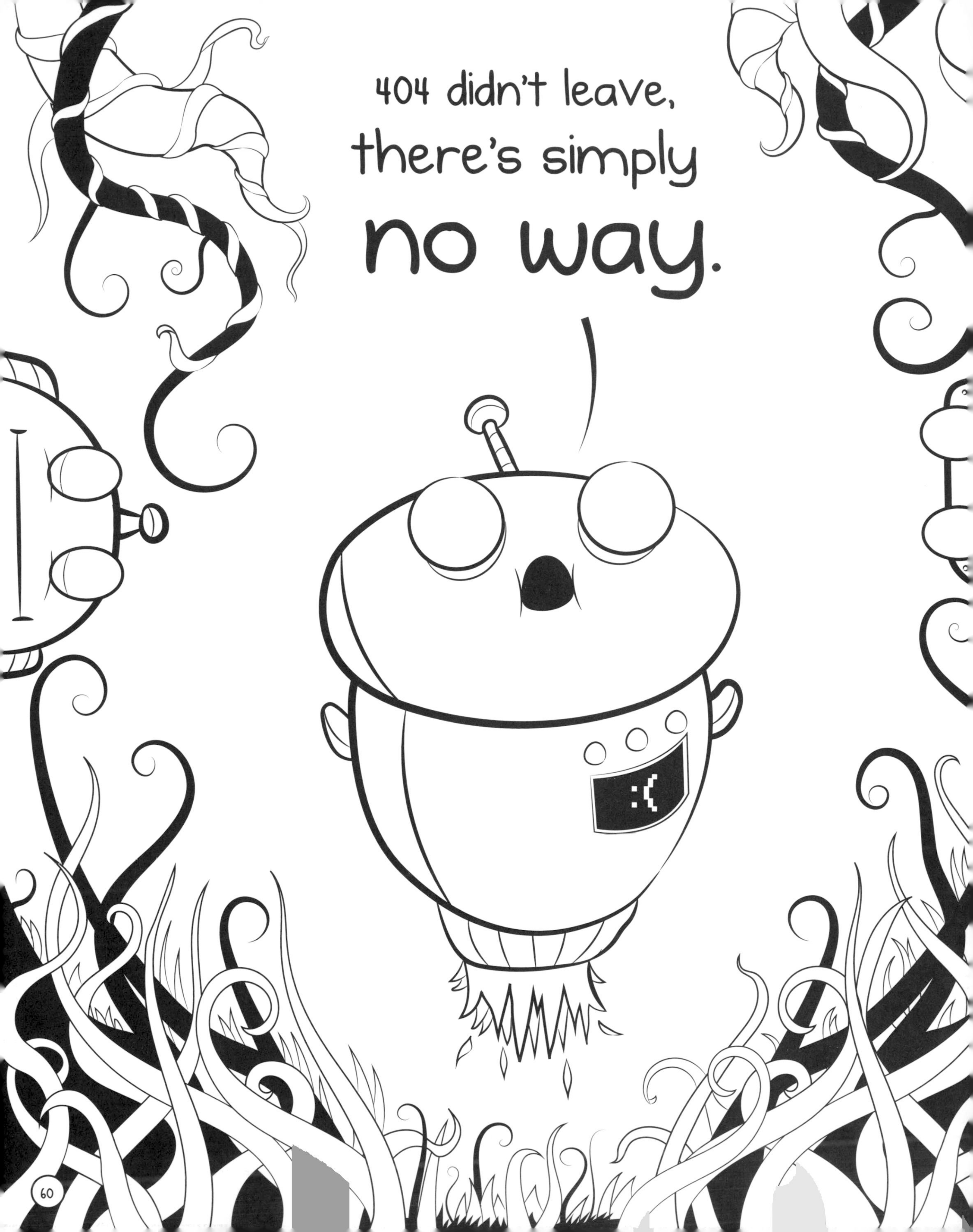
404 didn't leave,
there's simply
no way.
:(

Our robot cake alone

is reason to stay.

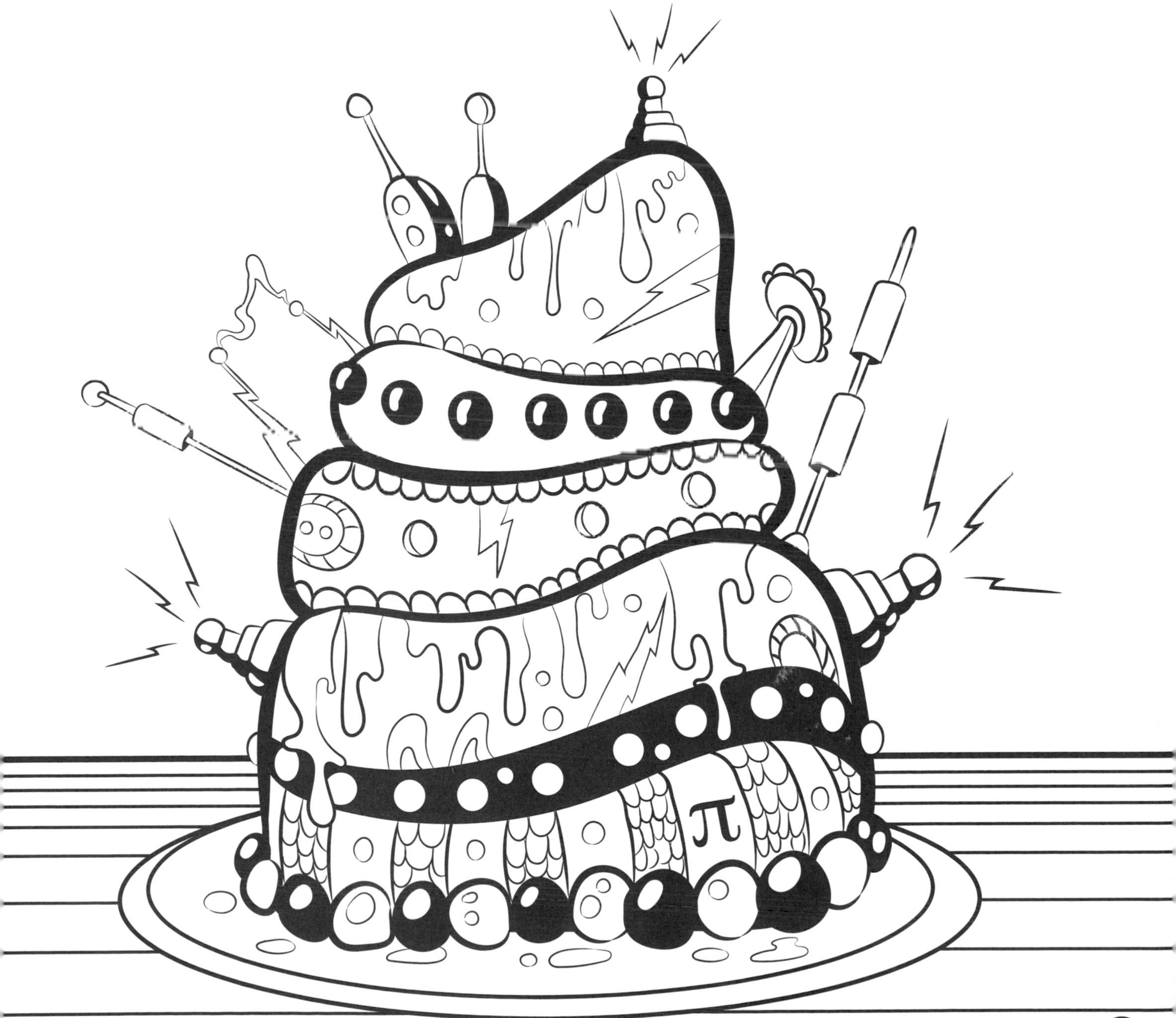

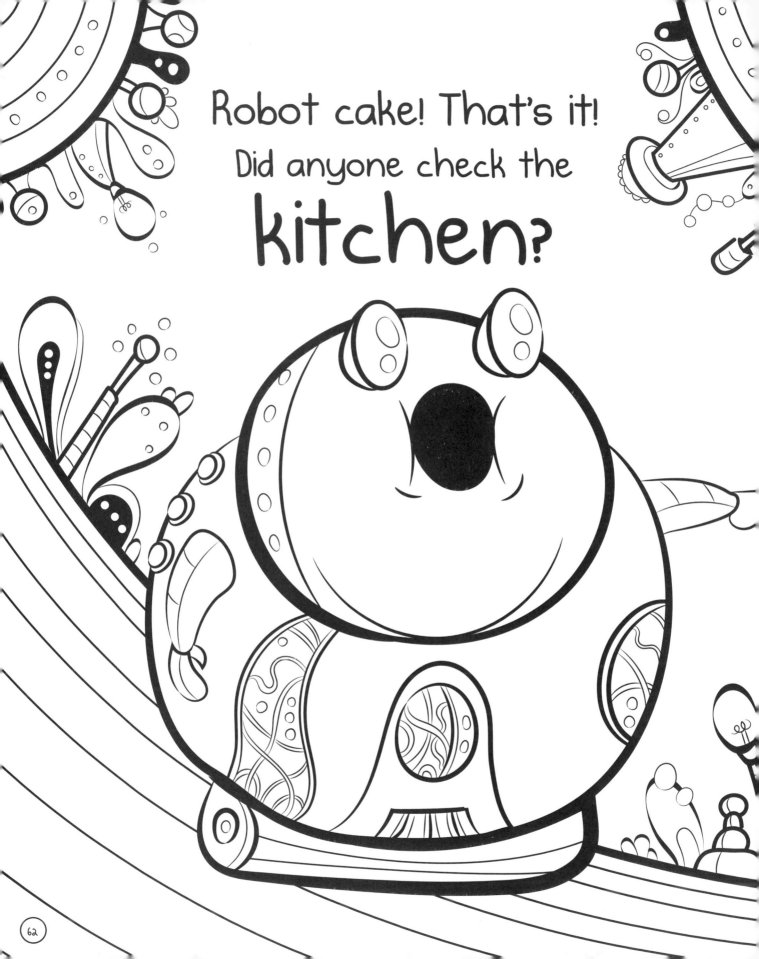

Robot cake! That's it!

Did anyone check the

kitchen?

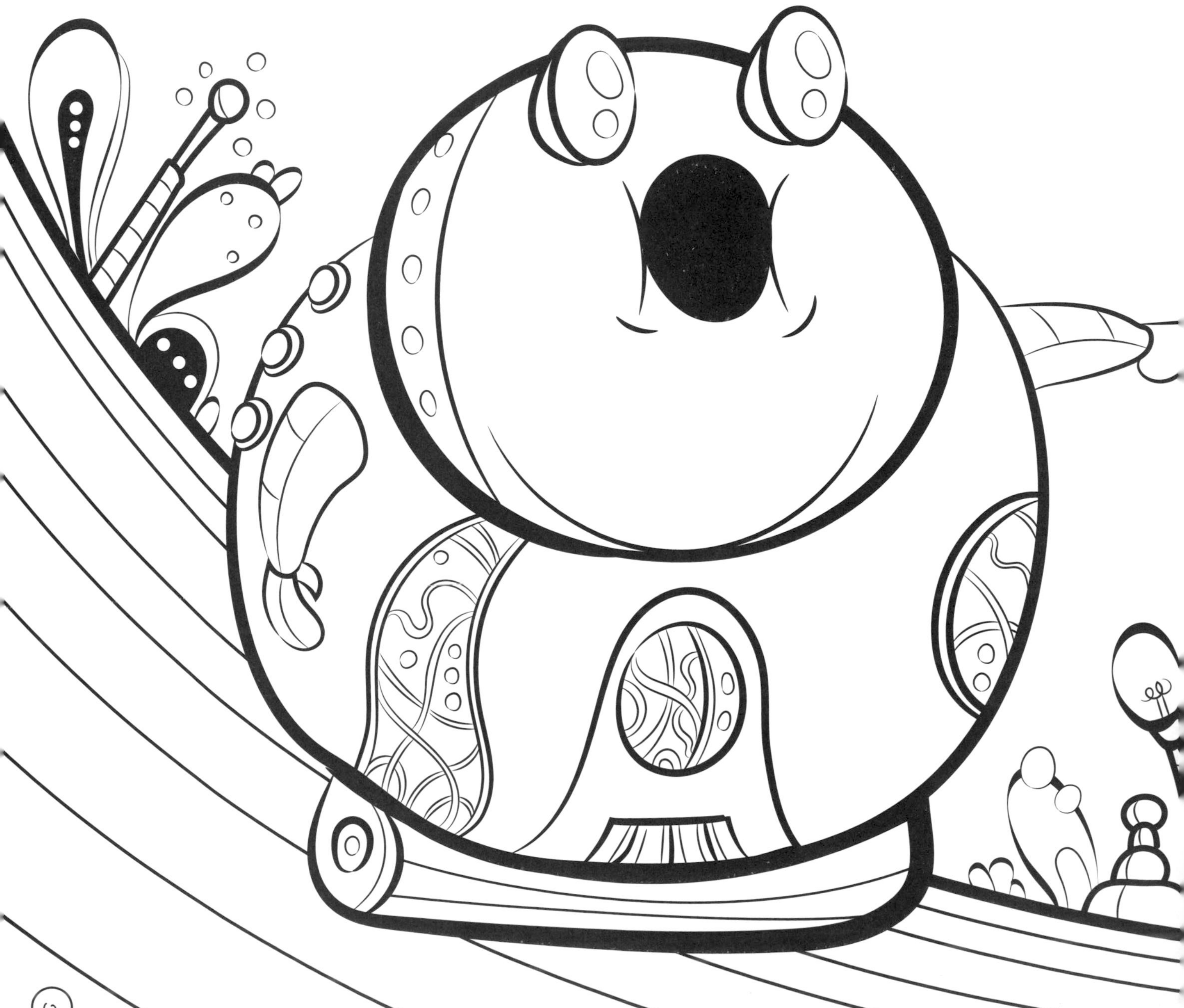

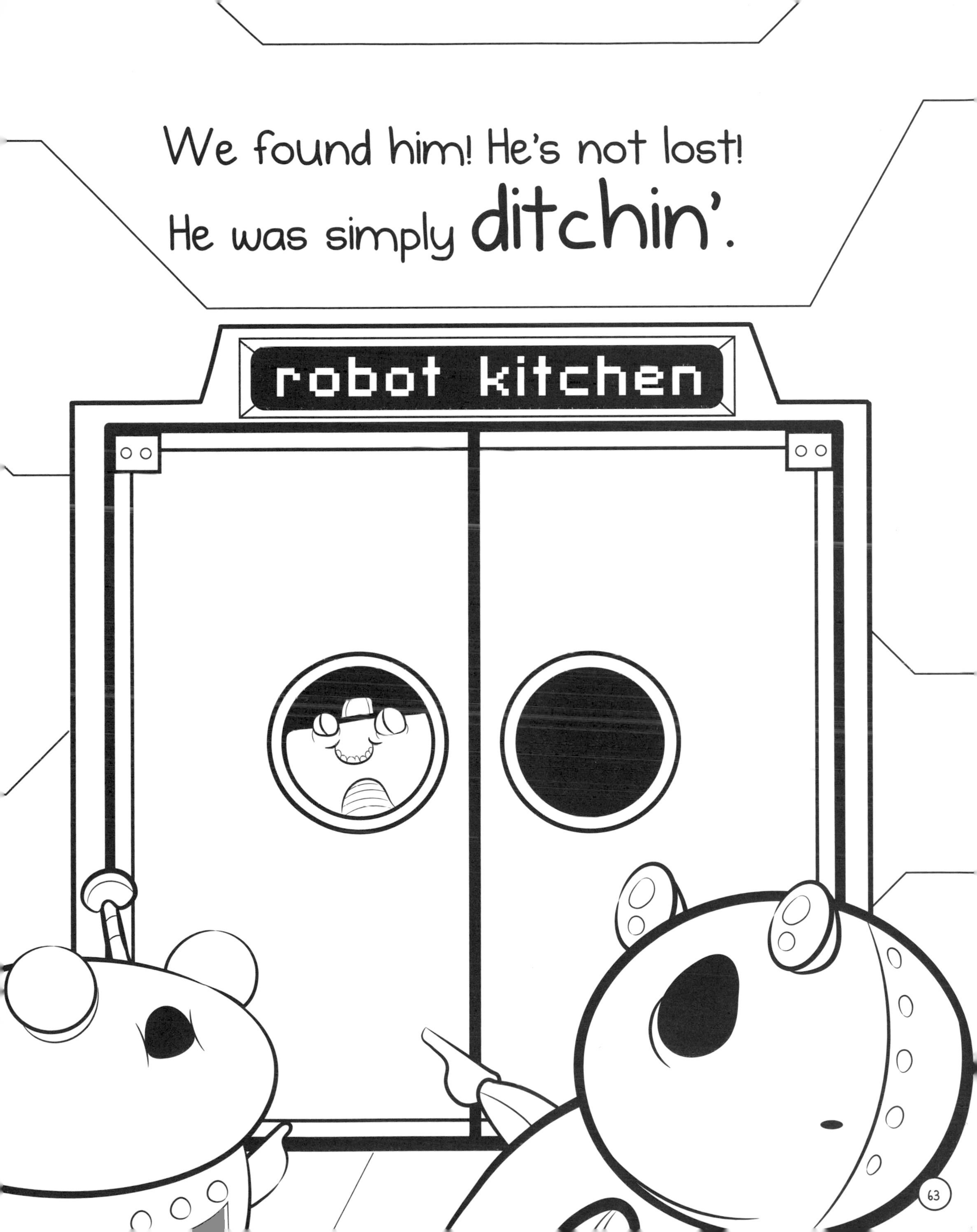
We found him! He's not lost!
He was simply ditchin'.
robot kitchen

404 isn't lost; he's found,

as found as can be.

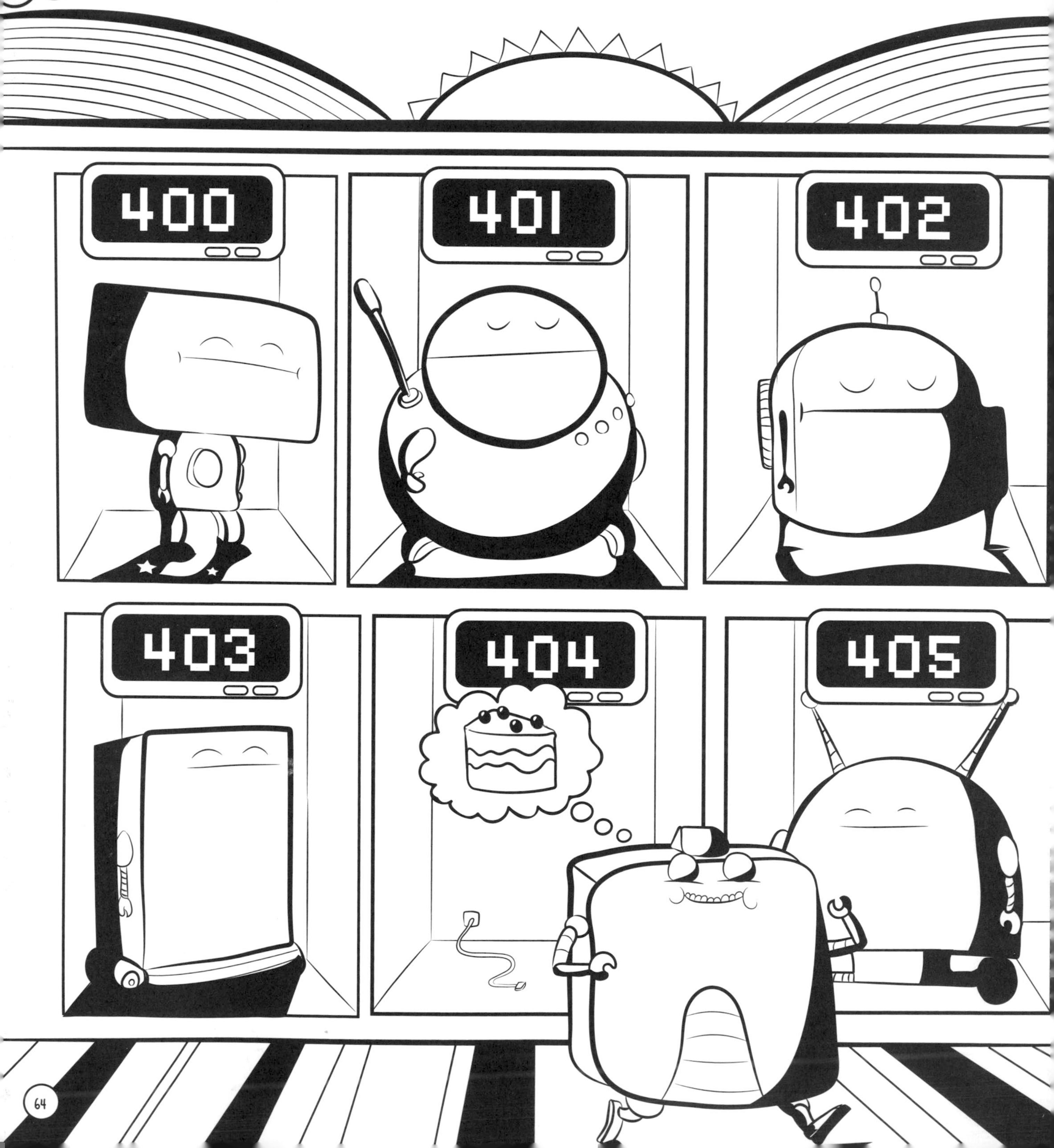

400
401
402
403
404
405

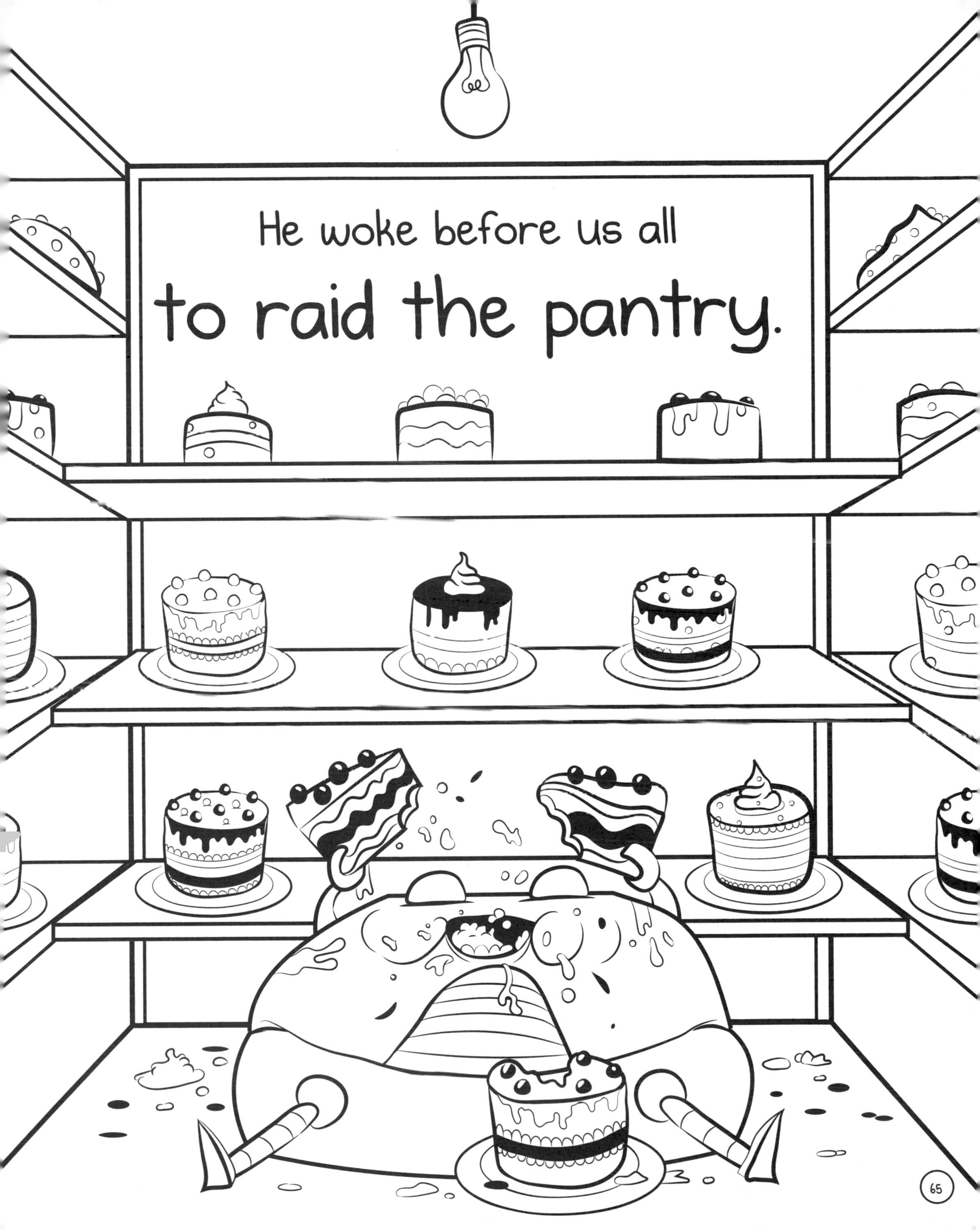
He woke before us all
to raid the pantry.

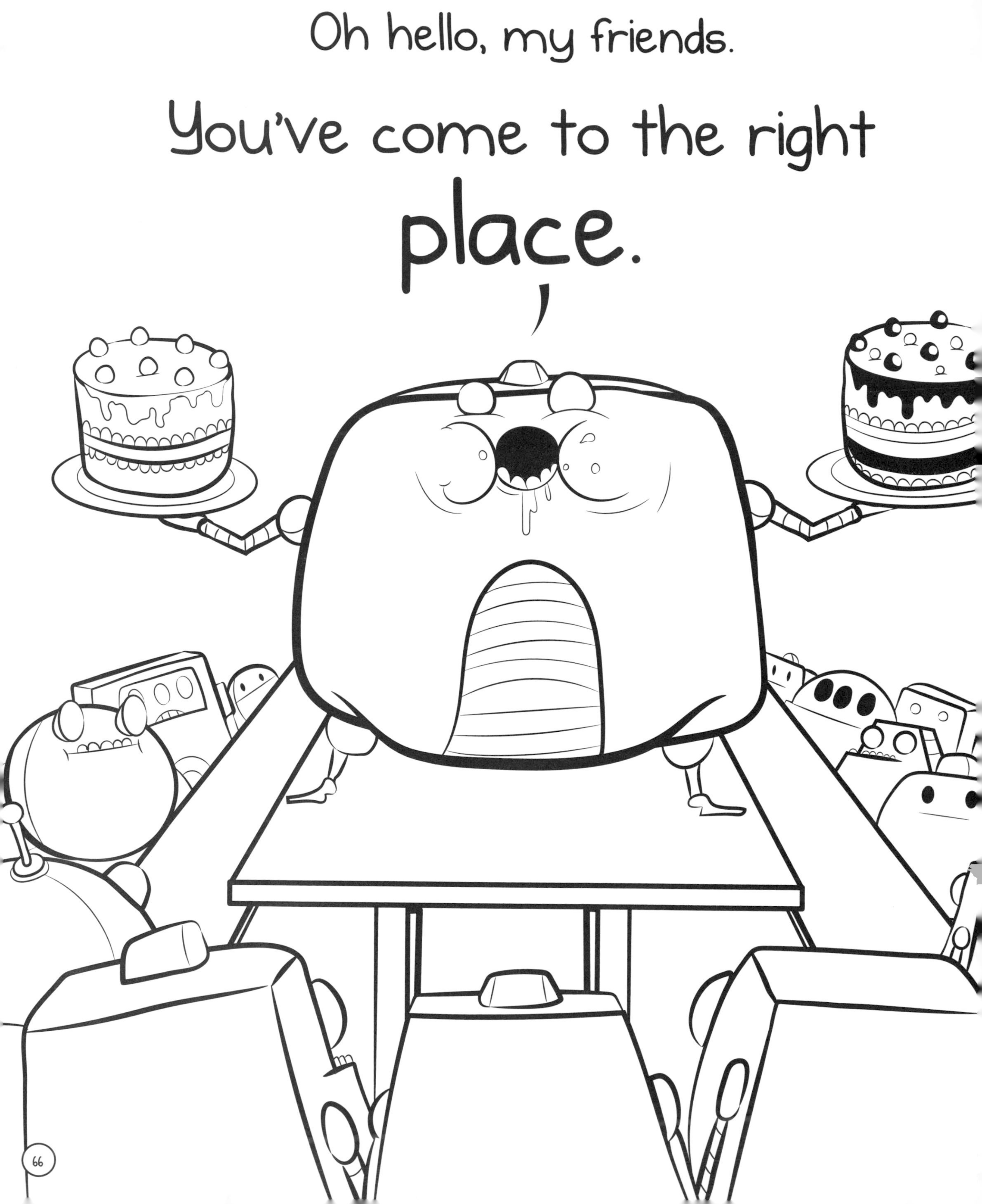
Oh hello, my friends.
You've come to the right
place.

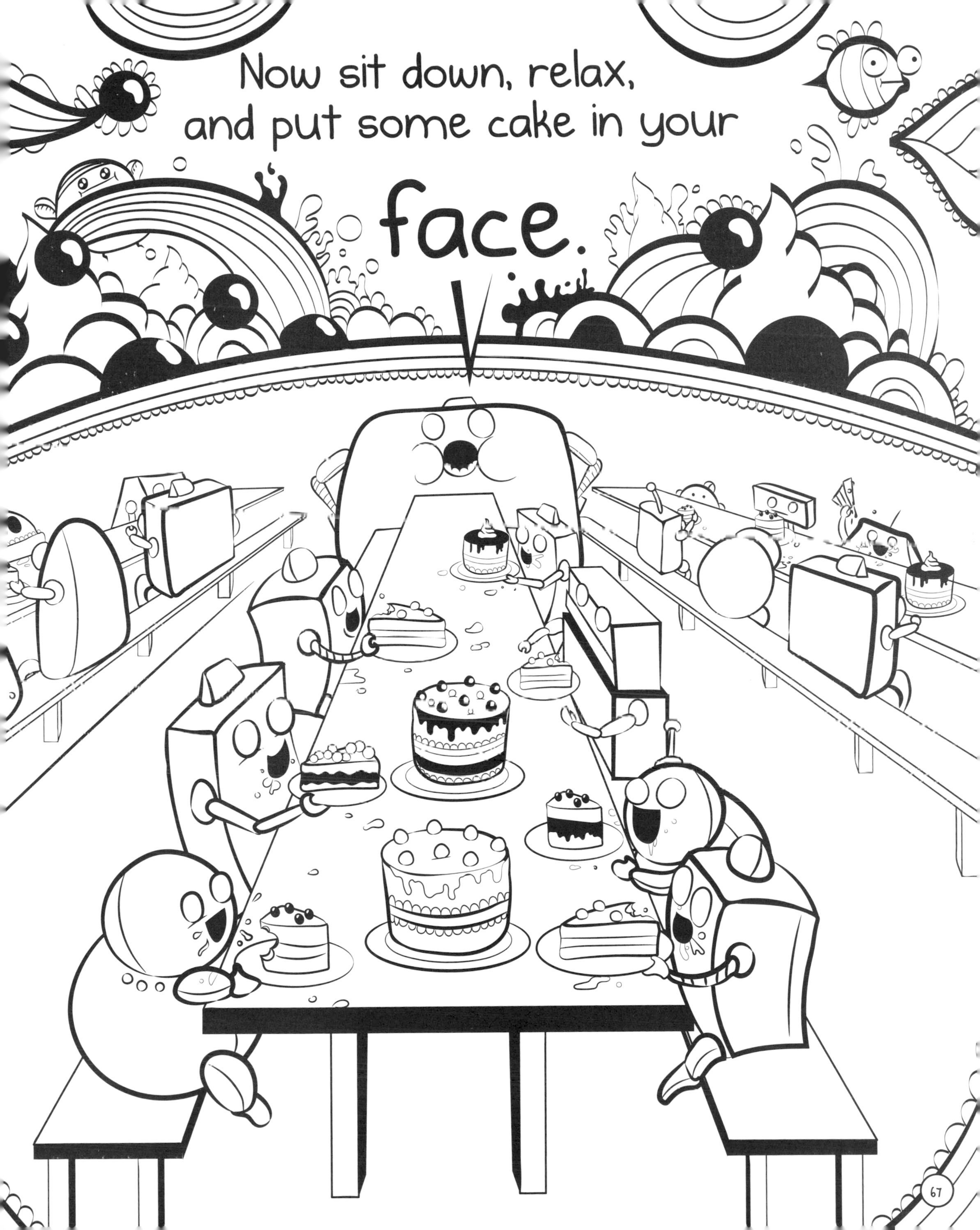
Now sit down, relax,
and put some cake in your
face.

The End.

Other books by The Oatmeal:

How to Tell If Your Cat
Is Plotting to Kill You

My Dog: The Paradox

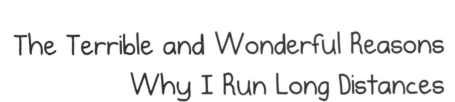

The Terrible and Wonderful Reasons
Why I Run Long Distances

Why Grizzly Bears
Should Wear Underpants

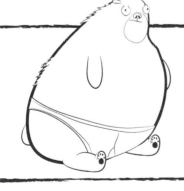

5 Very Good Reasons to
Punch a Dolphin in the Mouth

More comics can be found online at
{ www.TheOatmeal.com }

About the author

This book was written and drawn by

Matthew Inman,

AKA The Oatmeal.

Matthew lives in Seattle, Washington, where he spends a lot of time cartooning in his underwear.

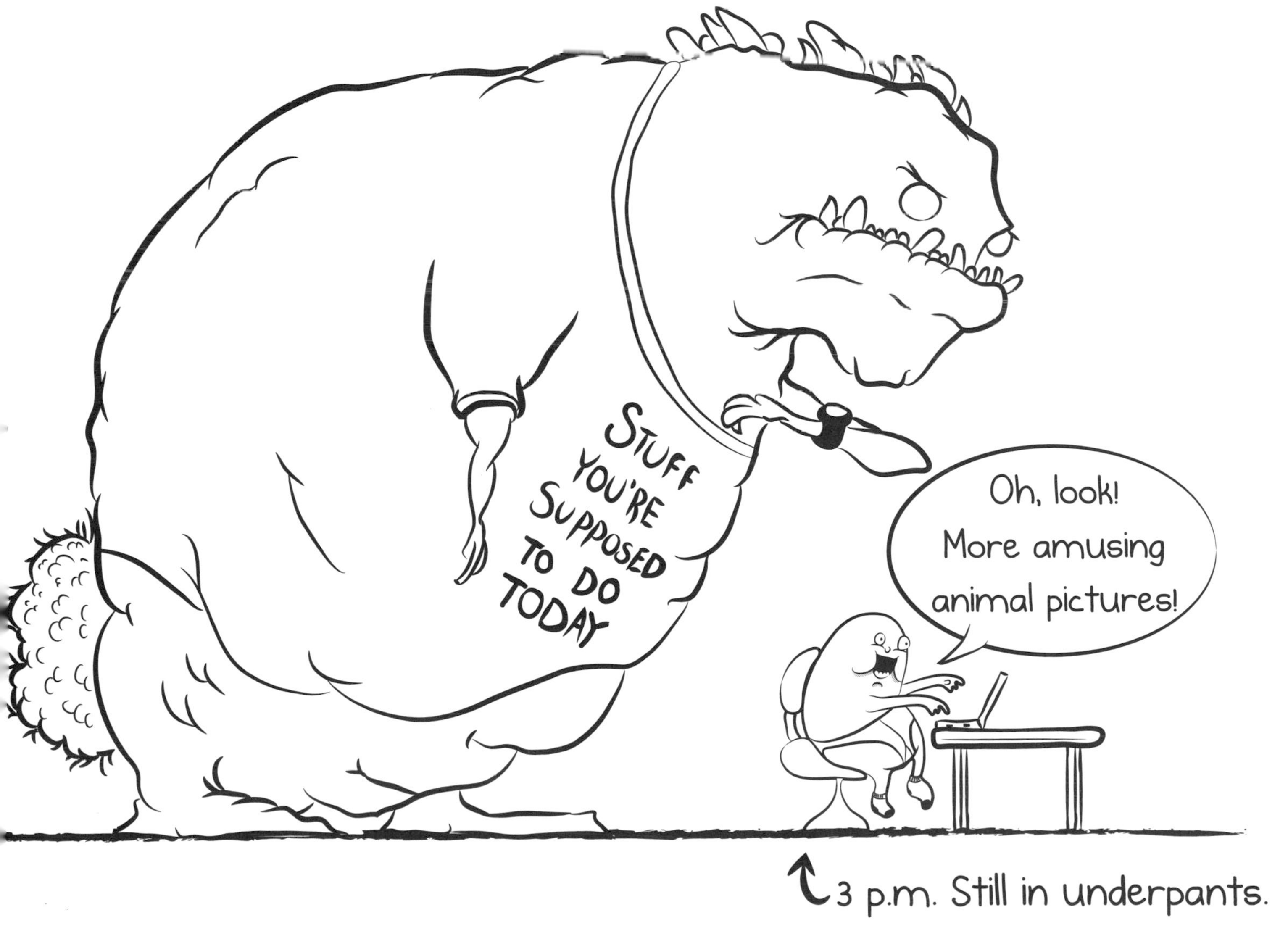
STUFF YOU'RE SUPPOSED TO DO TODAY
Oh, look! More amusing animal pictures!
3 p.m. Still in underpants.

404 not found

Andrews McMeel Publishing
a division of Andrews McMeel Universal
1130 Walnut Street, Kansas City, Missouri 64106

www.andrewsmcmeel.com

16 17 18 19 20 RRO 10 9 8 7 6 5 4 3 2 1

ISBN: 978-1-4494-8047-9

Editor: Patty Rice
Designer, Art Director: Diane Marsh
Production Manager: Cliff Koehler
Production Editor: Erika Kuster

ATTENTION: SCHOOLS AND BUSINESSES
Andrews McMeel books are available at quantity discounts with bulk purchase for educational, business, or sales promotional use. For information, please e-mail the Andrews McMeel Publishing Special Sales Department: specialsales@amuniversal.com.